THE
DIGITAL
NOMAD
HANDBOOK

Practical tips and inspiration for
living and working on the road

© GAUDILAB / SHUTTERSTOCK

CONTENTS

WHERE TO GO

BEFORE YOU GO

MAKING THE LEAP

HOW TO BE A DIGITAL NOMAD

INSPIRATION: DIGITAL NOMAD TALES

© STANISLAW PYTEL / GETTY IMAGES

MAKING THE LEAP

Are you a digital nomad?

Have you ever dreamed of packing in the nine-to-five and setting off on the road, with your laptop as your office and wherever you lay your hat as your home? Have you fantasised about filing invoices from the beach, writing reports from Rio or catching up with clients from a pavement cafe in a cobblestone square? If so, you're already part of the way down the road to becoming a digital nomad.

Sure, abandoning the comforts and security of home to start a new life as the ultimate free-wheeling freelancer might seem daunting, but thousands of others have been through the same doubts and uncertainties, and still made the decision to go. You'll never know if you don't try, and it might just be the start of a whole new way of living.

So why wait a moment longer? Turn the page, get inspired, and take the first steps to turn your dream of being a digital nomad into reality...
➵⟶

THE BENEFITS

THE OPPORTUNITIES

THE PRACTICALITIES

Who hasn't secretly dreamed of being their own boss? Setting your own schedule? Doing only what you want to do? Working when you want to work? As a digital nomad, you call the shots. If you want to work from a beach bungalow or a rainforest retreat, nobody can stop you. All you need is a laptop and a fast internet connection, and the world, or at least most of it, is your office.

Back home, you know exactly where the road goes, and what you'll find at the end of it. As a digital nomad, the future is unwritten and you can decide on the hoof where you go next and what you do when you get there. In the process, you'll learn more than you realise about running a business, taking charge of your own destiny and navigating your way around the world.

For all the perks, travelling and working as a location-independent freelancer has its challenges. Running your business from the road can mean long hours and financial uncertainty. You'll have to be jump-out-of-bed proactive about finding clients, chasing invoices and building your brand. Some days it will be just you and your laptop versus the world. So be ready for the highs and lows and you'll get the best out of the experience.

What's stopping you?

There are always a million reasons not to do something new and ambitious, but if everyone thought that way, there would be no space travel, no electric cars, and the world's greatest rock stars would still be serving cappuccinos at Starbucks. To overcome your doubts and fears, break things down into bite-sized chunks – taken individually, those insurmountable obstacles that were holding you back might be easier to conquer than you realise.

© HERO IMAGES / GETTY IMAGES

I'M NOT SURE I'M READY

Everyone feels this way before a major life change, but the only way to know is to try. Everyone who has ever achieved anything has felt moments of doubt along the way. But remember, you are the captain of this ship. You can decide when to go, where to go, and even – if things don't turn out quite as planned – when to turn back. To make things easier, begin with an easy destination, and a comfortable budget, and build in a breakpoint where you can decide whether to stop or continue.

I'M WORRIED ABOUT BURNING BRIDGES

© FRED FROESE / GETTY IMAGES

Making a change always means ending one thing and beginning another, but the same would be true for any new job. Remember nothing is forever – as master of your own destiny, you can continue for as long as you are enjoying the journey, and stop when you feel like stopping. And becoming a digital nomad doesn't mean ending existing relationships. Keep in touch regularly with friends, family and colleagues and you can bring your support network along for the ride.

WHAT IF I RUN OUT OF MONEY?

It's a valid worry on any trip, but take away the stress by building up a comfortable buffer before you step into the unknown. Save while you are working to clear any debts, and build a nest egg that you can dip into in an emergency to cover any gaps between payments. Set some ground rules; know how much money you need, how long you need it to last, and how low your funds can go before you need to do something radical. Even if you end up coming home, there's nothing to stop you trying again at a later point in time.

I'M NOT USED TO BEING ON MY OWN

Starting any solo journey can be daunting, but setting off alone may be just the push you need to transform your dreams into reality. Travelling with someone else means compromise and sharing the decision making; as a solo traveller, you can change plans as needed to keep your trip on the rails. And solo travel doesn't have to mean being alone; through co-working and networking with other digital nomads, you'll build up a whole new network of friends and contacts.

I FEEL BAD ABOUT LEAVING FRIENDS & FAMILY

Leaving the ones you love is always a wrench, but thanks to apps such as Skype and WhatsApp, it has never been easier to stay in touch. Separation can put a strain on relationships, but plenty of people manage to overcome distance, and you may find your significant other ends up coming along for the ride, or you both set off together in an entirely new direction. And remember, there are no rules about being constantly on the road; you can always pop home for a holiday when the mood takes you.

WHAT IF I CAN'T GET ENOUGH WORK?

Every freelancer feels the same way, but once you've been doing it a while, you learn to adjust to operating without that full-time-job sense of security. And the more work you do for different clients, the easier it will be to pick up work in future. Always keep your 'shop window' – your website, blog, LinkedIn page and social media profiles – up to date, and use your expanding network to find new opportunities. And remember, you can always change direction; freelancing can actually be a stepping stone to a new, better job if you decide to hang up your boots for a little more security.

WHAT ABOUT MY CAREER?

Ask any HR professional and they'll tell you that a gap in your resume is only a problem if you can't explain what you did with your time. Many employers will see taking a break from full-time employment to start your own business as a sign of confidence, initiative and entrepreneurial spirit. Remember, part of the reason you became a digital nomad was because you wanted a change, and you may find that the experience takes you off in a whole new career direction. If you can keep doing freelance work for your old employer, even better; you'll be keeping the door open for a possible return if you decide you want a break from the peripatetic life.

There's a popular image of digital nomads as 20-something whizz-kids, running lifestyle blogs and jumping into jungle pools with GoPro cameras. It's not entirely inaccurate – many nomads are young entrepreneurs, using remote working as an alternative to the traditional gap-year, without the limitations of time and budget. However, plenty of nomads are older professionals, taking their considerable experience on the road in pursuit of their first love: travel. So long as you can work remotely over an internet connection, this is a job with no upper age limit!

AM I TOO OLD?

TEN PERKS OF BEING A DIGITAL NOMAD

There are myriad perks to being footloose and fancy-free and unbound by the ties of working for one employer in one location. Here are some of the top advantages to the digital nomad life.

1 CHOOSING YOUR OWN OFFICE

As a digital nomad, you choose where you work, whether that means a coffee shop, a co-working space, or a palm-thatched bungalow on a tropical beach. Numerous surveys have revealed that people feel happier with some variety in their working environment, rather than sitting every day doing the same thing in the exact same space.

2 CHOOSING YOUR OWN HOURS

While it takes some discipline to set your own hours and stick to a routine, as a digital nomad, how you structure your time is completely down to you. If you want to start the day with a scuba dive and clock on at midday, you can. If you want to sleep all day and work through the night, there's no-one stopping you.

3 MAXIMUM VARIETY

Nothing stifles creativity quite like doing the same thing over and over again. As a digital nomad, you'll be working on something new for every contract, sometimes for completely new people, and often in a completely new location. Freelancing is the embodiment of the maxim that variety is the spice of life!

4 NO MORE COMMUTING

Numerous surveys have shown that the daily commute is the number one hate for most workers. More than 50% of people resent the daily commute and the number is even higher for people working in big cities. For digital nomads, your commuting time is limited to the seconds it takes to walk over to the laptop and connect to the internet, so no more standing on the train or fighting through the turnstiles on the Underground.

5 MORE TIME FOR LEISURE

Less time commuting means more time for the fun things in life. Most digital nomads rate having more time for leisure as one of the top perks of the freelance life, and being somewhere interesting means maximum opportunities to do new and exciting things you've never done before. Keep play and work in balance and this could be a lifestyle that never needs to end.

6 LESS STRESS

Commuting isn't just tiring, it's draining. Around 20% of people cite commuting to work as the main cause of stress in their lives, while a similar number blame long working hours, and some 10% are stressed by office politics. Being a digital nomad means being your own boss, setting your own hours, and spending time with the people you like being around – or spending time by yourself whenever the fancy takes you.

7 NO DRESS CODE

Some people love wearing a suit; other people feel it's like school uniform for grown-ups. As a digital nomad, you can wear what you like, when you like, whether that's Gore-tex and snowshoes, board shorts and flip-flops or a made-to-measure three-piece suit from a Singaporean tailor.

8 PERSONAL DEVELOPMENT

Being able to choose your own direction means plenty of opportunities for personal development. You'll learn to be self-reliant and comfortable in your own company. You'll become more organised and more confident in your ability to rise to a challenge. And you'll learn what is really important in life, without other people's ideas and preconceptions clouding your judgement.

9 BUSINESS SKILLS 101

Working as a freelancer is a boot camp in the skills needed to run any business. You'll learn to manage your time and financial affairs, scout for new clients, stay on top of invoices and build a growing brand. Plenty of business-starters made the jump to creating their own empires after learning the ropes as a freelance sole trader.

10 SEE THE WORLD

As they used to say in the navy: become a digital nomad, see the world. With the wireless lifestyle made possible by digital technology, you can set up almost anywhere, and move camp when you fancy a change of scenery. Work in one place all year, or move with the changing seasons? Spend the week on the beach and weekends in the mountains? The choice really is yours.

HOW TO BE A
DIGITAL NOMAD

Top trades for digital nomads

You could travel right around the world without ever seeing a sign saying 'digital nomads wanted!' Being a digital nomad is a way of life, and an approach to keeping work and travel in harmonious balance, rather than a specific job description.

 ## PICKING A PROFESSION

Deciding how to make a living while you trot the globe is the biggest single decision you'll have to make as a digital nomad. Once you've cracked this all-important first step, additional details such as where to go and how to spend your time outside working hours are something you can work out at your own pace, perhaps under a palm tree, updating your blog while sipping a piña colada.

Start with what you know. It will almost always be easier to find work in a field where you already have years of experience. Speak to your current employer about freelance opportunities, and ask about referrals to other companies who may need your skills. Try to pick up your first pieces of freelance work while you are still working so you have a pipeline of projects ready for when you actually hit the road.

 ## JACK OR JILL OF ALL TRADES?

You don't have to be limited to just one thing. Plenty of digital nomads have several business ventures in play, mixing up creative endeavours with more financially secure work in IT, web-design and business support. Indeed, having more than one way of making money can make it much easier to find enough work and sustain the nomad lifestyle. And having something to fall back on is a useful security net in case your brilliant new blog takes longer than planned to get rolling.

The most important thing is to be clear in your messaging to clients. If your remote work is split between web-design and being an online language teacher, have more than one online profile, so that people looking for someone to design a website see you as a web-designer and students see you as a teacher. Don't be afraid to have multiple websites and multiple social media identities to emphasise different parts of your business.

BE READY TO PIVOT

Freelancing isn't the same as being an employee. You don't have an official job description, or a manager looking over your shoulder – so if something you do isn't working, change it. If you can't find enough clients for one part of your business, shift attention to areas that are making money. If a formerly successful venture dips, try something new.

Using your existing skills

Plenty of people become digital nomads for a change of pace, and in many cases this means a complete change of career. This is, after all, a chance for you to re-evaluate what you like and don't like doing, and what you want from life. However, there's no reason to throw your old resume on the bonfire. Many of the skills from your old job are just as marketable in the freelance world, and having multiple money-making opportunities can only be an asset as you start your remote-working journey.

Think about the aspects of your existing work that give you the most satisfaction and consider how to use the same skills in different ways to meet your travel goals. You may find that what you needed was not so much a change of career as a change of scenery, and the liberation of being your own boss.

USE YOUR NETWORK

WORK OUTSIDE THE BOX

KEEP YOUR SKILLS UP TO DATE

You already know plenty of people in your own industry, so approach contacts before you head off, either directly or via networking sites like LinkedIn. Let people know that you're going freelance and looking for work; you might be surprised how many have projects for a skilled individual such as yourself. And ask your contacts if they know anyone who's looking for freelancers – there's no shame in making use of your extended network to build a pool of clients.

'Existing skills' doesn't have to mean doing exactly what you've been doing day in, day out in the office for the last seven years. Most people have a string of talents that could be leveraged to make money while they travel. Do you play guitar? Why not offer online lessons? Are you fully in tune with the latest wellness trends? Start a blog about it. Do you have language teaching experience? Take it online via video streaming.

Being a freelancer puts your talents on full display, and there's no HR department to turn to when you need to brush up your skills. Consider taking refresher courses before you set off, so your business skills are in tune with what clients are currently looking for. And keep an eye out for new skills that could grow your business once you're on the road; many co-working spaces offer training in key skills for digital nomads, so you can regularly top up your resume while you travel.

TOP TIP

'It's tempting to get sidetracked chasing what you see other digital nomads doing. Ignore the shiny objects and double down on skills you already have. The success of a digital nomad is directly proportional to their ability to find a niche. While it shouldn't stop you from learning new skills or diversifying income streams, the strengths you already have are often your greatest asset.'

Josh Summers, director, www. travelchinacheaper.com.

© WESTEND 61 / GETTY IMAGES

What jobs do digital nomads do?

Some jobs seem tailor-made for a nomadic lifestyle. If you are already set on jetting around the planet, becoming a travel blogger and writing about your journey seems like a no-brainer. But plenty of other jobs and trades slot neatly into the location-independent lifestyle. The key criteria for digital nomads is being able to do the actual day-to-day work from wherever you happen to be in the world, via the medium of a high-speed internet connection.

 **A WORLD OF CODE**

Travel blogging may have the glamour, but plenty of digital nomads make better money, and fund a more luxurious lifestyle, by being part of that select group who speak the universal language of computer code. Freelancing is the cornerstone of the software development business, and travellers who can code in desirable languages, such as Java, Python, C++, Javascript and SQL will find their skills are in demand wherever they happen to be in the world. And did we mention web design? Or did you think that the person who designed your website was working from an office in Dunstable?

 **CREATIVE ENDEAVOURS**

Blogging isn't the only creative activity that can fund your travels. Many digital nomads turn to other kinds of writing – from on-message travel writing to more prosaic scribing such as writing advertising copy, authoring manuals for appliances or writing training materials for office tasks you've actually left far behind. Don't forget editing, one of the most portable professions around. Then there's the visual sphere: graphic design, videography, photography, layout. If you don't have to be in a specific place when you do it, almost any creative activity can form the foundation of a digital nomad life.

 **TAKE YOUR JOB WITH YOU**

Many of the day-to-day tasks that keep a business going don't actually have to take place in the office. Managing projects, supervising social media, doing the accounts – all things that can be done from a pavement cafe with a fast wi-fi connection. Even one-time face-to-face jobs, such as working as an office assistant, have moved into the virtual sphere. In fact, almost anything that can be done in an office can now be done remotely if you can find a client willing to pay you for the service.

TEN TOP DIGITAL NOMAD JOBS

1 **Software developer**
Remote working is a standard part of development, so it's a small leap to being a coding nomad.

2 **Web designer**
A perfectly portable profession, where what matters to clients is results, not where you are based.

3 **Travel Blogger**
Writing about your travels to pay for your travels is a perfect partnership.

4 **Language Teacher**
Thanks to distance learning over the internet, the world is your classroom.

5 **SEO Specialist**
Learn how to optimise content for search engines and make money helping companies up their game.

6 **Social Media Expert**
Managing social media accounts is a business that works from anywhere.

7 **Technical Support Representative**
You don't have to be physically in the room to keep tech ticking over smoothly.

8 **Virtual Assistant**
Companies need remote support in everything from accounts and invoicing to project management.

9 **Freelance Writer**
Writing is one of the most portable ways of making a living, whether you blog about wellness or write manuals for microwaves.

10 **Graphic Designer**
Some simple tech can transform your laptop into a portable design studio.

TEACH THE WORLD

Remember the days when the only way to learn something was to traipse into a classroom or pick up a 'Teach Yourself...' book from the local library? No, neither do we. In the digital age, a huge amount of what we learn takes place in the digital space, from online music tutorials to workplace subconscious bias training and videos to improve your knowledge of SEO. With a fast web connection and a quality webcam, you can impart your knowledge to paying students almost anywhere in the world.

START FROM THE GROUND FLOOR

Launching a start-up might seem like a big step, but household names such as Uber, eBay and Facebook all began life as one person with tech experience and a smart idea. If you've got a model for an online business that could revolutionise the way we live our lives, you'll be one of a growing contingent of digital nomads pursuing the same dream. Moving in a world of co-working spaces and networking meetups, you'll have plenty of encounters with fellow entrepreneurs, and the opportunity to share ideas, forge new business relationships, and perhaps even build the dream team who go on to become the next online superstars.

Become a travel blogger

On the face of it, travelling and working as a travel blogger seems like a match made in heaven. You're already travelling. You're having amazing experiences. You've got something new to add to your blog every day. And you're living the dream, working while travelling the world, so there must be millions of people out there itching to hear about it? The only problem is that thousands of other travellers have exactly the same idea.

With the easy availability of free blogging software and online tutorials, setting up a blog is within reach of even the most tech-skeptical traveller, and the internet is buzzing with blogs covering every imaginable aspect of travel, and every imaginable destination. To make a blog that stands out, attracts a following and, most importantly of all, makes money, requires hard work, dedication and a little bit of luck. The Field of Dreams attitude of 'build it and they will come' is not how things really work, except for a lucky few.

 ## FIRST STEPS

You'll almost certainly find it easier if you don't start out relying 100% on your blog as your only source of money. Having a second income stream – be it programming, photography, web design, consulting or some other kind of writing – will take the pressure off your blog, giving you time to build your travel brand intelligently and establish paying relationships with sponsors and advertisers.

Every travel blogger is competing for the same traffic, so think from the beginning about what makes your blog stand out from the pack. Having a Unique Selling Proposition (USP) is a key step toward gathering followers and attracting advertiser interest. Go online and see what competitors are doing, and think about what you could do differently.

 ## PLAY TO YOUR STRENGTHS

Do you have any specialist knowledge that might appeal to people with similar interests? Is there a certain niche that you feel particularly passionate about? The most successful blogs are quite specific, rather than trying to be all things to all people. If you set up a blog covering photography, Shetland ponies and bungee jumping, you'll struggle with SEO, and advertisers will struggle to see how your blog is relevant to the products they are trying to sell.

TOP 5 BLOGGING PLATFORMS

The days when a blog could be pasted together like a student newspaper are long gone. Today's internet users expect blogs to look and feel professional, as well as delivering great content that they absolutely have to read. Here are the most popular platforms for launching a new blog.

Wordpress.org

The world's most popular blogging platform, Wordpress powers 30% of sites on the internet. It's free, though you have to host the software on your own site, which means paying for a domain name and website hosting. Once you've mastered the basics, Wordpress can be used for anything from a bare-bones travel blog to a commercial business portal, and plug-ins add smart functionality, such as easy monitoring of SEO (Search Engine Optimisation) and the ability to add images to tweets about your blog entries. Customisable themes make it easy to create a standout look, and adding forums or an online shop is also a doddle. The downside is that you have to manage your own site, including installing updates and running backups, and it takes time to learn how to get the best out of the software; www.wpbeginner. com is a good place to start.

Wordpress.com

If going under the bonnet and doing your own web design sounds like too much work, Wordpress offers an all inclusive hosting service, with the option of a free site, if you don't mind living with limited whistles and bells and a Wordpress domain name, such as website.wordpress. com. If you want to run your own advertising and have more options for customising your site, you can upgrade to a personal plan for US$4 to US$36 per month, depending on how many features you need. This also gets you a personal domain name and removes all the Wordpress branding. A Wordpress.com site is a solid base for first timers, but technically savvy nomads can do more with the locally hosted version of Wordpress.

© ALEXANDER SPATARI / GETTY IMAGES

Gator

www.hostgator.com/website-builder

Gator is a website builder and blogging platform run by Houston-based company HostGator, who also host websites based on other platforms. While not as versatile and customisable as Wordpress, the drag-and-drop interface is great for nomads building a website for the very first time, and hosting plans include a free personal domain name and SSL certificate, and website admin such as regular backups and security checks. Annual plans for building and hosting your website range from US$4 to UD$9 per month, depending on how many commercial features you need. It's perhaps the fastest way to get a brand new site on the web, but you don't have access to such a wide range of apps and add-ons.

Blogger

www.blogger.com

With a Google account, you can get on board the blogging bandwagon for free using this simple, and easy-to-manage interface run by Google. On the plus side, it's secure and easy to use; on the downside, it's quite old technology, and not as dynamic and customisable as Wordpress, and you'll have a blogspot.com domain name unless you buy your own domain from a third-party registrar. Overall, it's an easy option for first timers starting out small, but if your blog grows, you might need to move to a more feature-rich environment on another platform.

Constant Contact

www.constantcontact.com/website/builder

Another beginner-friendly website builder and hosting service, with a feature-packed free hosting service that you can try before you sign up to the full package. As well as customisable templates and drag-and-drop design, you get access to a library of 550,000 free images to add colour and pizazz to your site. And the engine is AI driven, which means it can do smart things such as self-populate with data from your Facebook page. Your site even comes with its own metrics dashboard, domain name and SSL certificate. After 60 days though, you'll need to sign up to a plan, with prices starting from US$18 or US$40 per month, depending on the features needed.

MAKING YOUR BLOG STAND OUT

With every traveller and their dog broadcasting their travel thoughts to the world, you'll need to go the extra mile to make your travel blog stand out from the pack. Here are a few tips.

Put yourself in the frame
Don't be generic; be personal. Share your thoughts and feelings. The more personality you put into your blog, the more it will stand out from the hundreds of rivals.

Interact
Engage with your readers. Allow visitors to comment and join in the discussion, giving readers a reason to come back to see where the conversation goes to next. Tweet about your latest postings on social media, and invite guest bloggers and experts to contribute to the pieces you are writing.

Find an angle
'My experiences as a solo woman traveller' has more immediacy than 'What I did on holiday'. Readers want content that speaks to them personally; think about what your personality, interests and expertise bring to the conversation.

Go beyond the obvious
Even when you cover the most obvious sights, try to find something new to say that hasn't been said a hundred times before. Can you find a new way to explore a familiar sight? Or a new angle to escape the tired travel clichés? If you can frame the experience through an interesting detail or a quirky piece of history, it can add a human element to your narrative.

Use good design
A blog doesn't have to have a million whistles and bells to keep readers coming back for more. Clean, uncluttered design and simple, intuitive navigation will win you more followers than a blog that turns backflips every time readers click on a new page.

Use amazing images
It should go without saying, but a picture is worth a thousand words. At the very least, a stunning photo will keep people on your site long enough to read the thousand words of amazing copy that you wrote to go alongside it. If you write about an amazing experience on your blog, you'll bring more readers along for the ride if you can show it with an image or video clip.

Post regularly
Give your followers a reason to come back. Rather than lavishing all your efforts into one show-stopping post once a year, say a little, often, mixed in with more substantial blocks of content. Combine in-depth themed features with smaller opinion pieces and observations to keep readers engaged.

PROMOTING YOUR BLOG

Nobody will notice all your great content unless you scream and shout about it. Publicising your blog is an essential tool for gaining followers and creating enough of a buzz for advertisers to want to get involved – as anyone building a road knows, it's all about traffic.

Be SEO friendly

Search Engine Optimisation (SEO) is crucial in getting your blog to climb search engine rankings. Ensure all your posts contain metadata, keywords and both external and internal links, and use an SEO plug-in like Yoast (www.yoast.com) for Wordpress to monitor how pages are tracking. Large images and video files can slow your site down, so use free apps such as JPEGMini (www. jpegmini.com) to shrink files without losing quality.

Give users what they want

Watching how users behave on your site can reap dividends. Tools such as Google Analytics (https://analytics.google.com) help you track the content that performs best and the subjects that resonate with readers, so you can consistently give users what they are looking for. Do some keyword research using Google's Keyword Planner, accessible via https://ads.google.com, to find keywords that are likely to generate clicks.

Add subscribers

Make it easy for people to return to your blog by inviting them to become subscribers. You'll soon build a mailing list, and letting people know when something new appears on the site will bring a surge of visits each time you post. Enable easy subscription with one-click checkboxes, and reward subscribers with bonus content that isn't available to ordinary users.

Get the word out on social media

Promote each new post on Twitter, Instagram, Facebook and other social channels, and make it easy for users to share your content with plug-ins that add automatic social media buttons to your pages. Tag your posts with hashtags on relevant subjects to get your content in front of new people. Remember to share content from other people (including other bloggers) so they feel inclined to share content from you!

Build relationships

Invite other bloggers to guest post on your site, and offer your services to others for free in exchange for a link back to your site. This kind of partnership is a great way for both sites to grow referral traffic, without any money changing hands. Connect with potential partners via social media, online forums and by connecting directly through LinkedIn and other industry channels.

MAKING MONEY FROM YOUR BLOG

Your blog can be a great place to show off your talents to potential clients, but with rent and co-working membership fees to consider, a blog that doesn't make money is just a diary. Making it pay is vital to funding your travels, particularly if you plan to blog full-time.

Advertising

If your site has plenty of visitors, you have a business proposition to put to advertisers. Cost Per Click (CPC) and Cost Per Thousand Impressions (CPM) advertisements rely on high traffic; both pay a fee every time users click or view the ads on your site. Google AdSense (www.google.com/adsense) adds a site banner that Google fills with ads related to your content; similar programmes are run by Infolinks (www.infolinks.com) and Media.net (www.media.net). You can also sell your own ad space, going directly to companies selling products and services, but advertisers will want to see proof of traffic numbers.

© OLEKSANDRA NAUMENKO / SHUTTERSTOCK

© MARTIN-DM / GETTY IMAGES

Affiliate marketing

Many bloggers boost revenue through affiliate marketing, where companies give a (small) cut when people buy their products via your site. This usually involves promoting through banner ads or links within your content. How much you endorse third-party products will depend on where you draw the line between editorial and ads. Too much affiliate marketing can create the impression that you'll push anything for cash, undermining your authority. Amazon Associates (www.affiliate-program.amazon.com) is one of the biggest programmes.

Sell something

As a digital nomad, you probably don't have the infrastructure to sell hard-copy printed books, but there's nothing to stop you selling ebooks, online courses, podcasts and training workshops; or apps, plug-ins, images, video and music that you create. You'll cut out the intermediary and keep all the profits, and this sideline could take on a life of its own. Consider selling paid subscriptions to specialist areas of your site, offering bonus content that has real value to subscribers (this works best for business blogs or instructional blogs that teach users new skills).

Other kinds of writing

Writing a travel blog might be the first thing that leaps to mind for peripatetic wordsmiths, but other kinds of writing can be just as rewarding, both emotionally and financially. Every word you've ever seen in print was written by someone.

Getting started

Starting out as a writer can be tough. Editors rarely respond to pitches unless they plan to commission, and many pitches are deleted without ever being read. It can be demoralising to know your artfully crafted ideas are going straight in the recycle bin, but once you have a few published pieces under your belt, you'll find editors more willing to engage with you. Visit the Write Life (www.thewritelife.com) and Freelance Writing (www.freelancewriting.com) for listings of publications that source content from freelancers.

© SOLOVYOVA / ISTOCK / GETTY IMAGES

Writing for newspapers & magazines

The primary obstacle to making money from travel writing is the cost of travelling, but as a digital nomad, you have the travel part covered. Most travel magazines and newspapers rely on a steady stream of articles from trusted contributors, but it's a crowded marketplace, so you need good ideas and a writing style that works for your target publication's readership. Find publications worldwide at OnlineNewpaperList (www.onlinenewspaperlist.com). Once you find a publication that appeals, browse past issues to get a flavour for their content and editorial slant, and check your pitch isn't for a destination covered recently. Check online for instructions on how to pitch, and find the specific editor to contact (pitches to generic addresses often go straight to the recycle bin). Mention your credentials when you pitch, and link to your website, blog or LinkedIn account.

Writing for websites

Most printed magazines run just a handful of freelance-sourced stories per edition, but online travel websites have an insatiable appetite for content, though rates of pay can be low compared to traditional print media. Sites such as The Culture Trip (www.theculturetrip.com) publish incredible numbers of articles to be shared via social media. However, be wary of 'content mill' sites who dangle the promise of large volumes of work but offer minimal rates of pay per article; few writers make money this way.

Writing for guidebooks

Guidebooks are the holy grail of travel writing. Contracts provide several months of guaranteed income, and few gigs offer the same chance to get under a destination's skin. Some publishers, including Lonely Planet, pay all expenses; others expect you to get freebies from tourist offices, travel agencies and hotels. You'll be gathering a lot of dry information (bus times, opening hours) as well as being paid to see the sights: be ready for hard graft. After a day of reviewing twenty almost identical hotels, you'll sometimes wonder if this was what you signed up for!

Most publishers have a network of trusted contributors; new writers will need particular regional expertise and a proven track record of writing great copy. Check publisher websites for openings.

Writing manuals

Every piece of equipment sold anywhere has a manual that was written by somebody. Manual writing – often known as a technical writing – can be handy work if you have industry knowledge and the ability to translate complicated technical ideas into simple, easy-to-digest instructions. Other technical writing jobs include creating training tools for business processes, or industry-focused training courses. Check freelance work sites such as Flexjobs (www.flexjobs.com), Upwork (www.upwork.com), Freelancer (www.freelancer.com) and People Per Hour (www.peopleperhour.com) for job listings.

Get ahead in online advertising

Online advertising is one of the main ways companies promote products; opportunities for remote work in the industry include copywriting and project management. To get ahead, it pays to have already worked in online ads – build up a freelance client pool before you head off. Your blog or website should show off your copywriting and SEO skills. Start looking for gigs through LinkedIn as well as Freelancer (www. freelancer.com), Upwork (www.upwork.com) and Creativepool (www.creativepool.com).

Editing

Pretty much every company that hires writers also has work for editors. With the right skills, it's easy to pick up remote editing work – everything from novels and travel guidebooks to company reports. Most companies have an in-house editing test, so swot up first via online assessments – the Society for Editors & Proofreaders (www.sfep.org.uk), Writing English (www. writingenglish.com) and ProEdit (www.proedit.com) have useful resources. Find gigs through sites such as Upwork (www.upwork.com), Flexjobs (www.flexjobs. com) and Fiverr (www.fiverr.com), and specialist editing sites such as Scribbr (www.scribbr.com).

Become an influencer?

Through hard work, tireless self promotion, smart networking and luck, influencers have made millions selling aspirational images and lifestyles. Most income comes from advertising, but if you're associated with a niche area, and can stay on message 100% of the time, brands may hire you as an ambassador, opening up lucrative sponsorship deals.

Show what you know

There's no such thing as a general influencer. Successful influencers find a niche that is perfectly in tune with their interests and expertise, usually within the industry they already work in. People turn to influencers for knowledge, advice, and reams of topic-specific content, so think about the target audience for everything you post.

Choose a platform

The favourite platform for influencers is Instagram, because it operates on a visual basis, providing maximum exposure for advertisers, but there are plenty of influencers on Twitter, Facebook and YouTube. To stand a chance of making money, you need massive traffic, so a big chunk of your time will be spent building and nurturing your follower base.

Find a unique voice

A big part of most influencers' brand is their personality: being somebody people trust and look up to. Projecting an image is part of the package – but don't be afraid to voice your own opinions; be honest about your successes and failures and you'll go further than someone who only tells people what they want to hear.

Network, network, network

Networking is at the heart of being a successful influencer, so connect with as many people as possible, in as many ways as possible. Engage with your followers, industry experts, other influencers and advertisers, and share freely and often. Buzzsumo (www.buzzsumo.com) is a handy way to find key influencers and the most shared posts.

SIX TRAVEL INFLUENCERS TO FOLLOW

To point you in the right direction, here are some of the top influencers on social media.

Murad Osmann (www.instagram.com/muradosmann) Lavish air-brushed images of travel that seem tailor-made for ad campaigns.

Tara Whiteman (www.instagram.com/taramilktea) Influencing as you've probably imagined it: lifestyle, luxury and fashion mag-worthy photos.

Chris Burkard (www.instagram.com/chrisburkard) A gifted surf photographer, filling his feed with stunning images of locations.

Jack Morris (www.instagram.com/doyoutravel) Selling travel and youth as lifestyle – all glamour, all the way.

The Bucket List Family (www.instagram.com/thebucketlistfamily) Making travel a family affair, full of Instagram instant glam.

Louis Cole (www.instagram.com/funforlouis) Feeds full of adrenaline activities and globetrotting travel experiences.

Code your way round the world

Thanks to real-time communication tools such as Slack (www.slack.com), Trello (www.trello.com) and Google Meet (https://meet.google.com), software development has moved out of the office onto the cloud, and a huge amount of the behind-the-scenes work that keeps the world's most popular apps and websites in operation is done by freelancers, many of them working from co-working spaces around the globe.

Speak the right language

An early decision to make when branching out into freelancing is whether to market yourself as a general coder, or focus on a specific niche. Being an expert on an industry-specific application for Kotlin, Javascript or Python can open up access to higher-paid gigs with less competition. On the other hand, having a broader range of skills can mean a wider choice of projects to apply for. Being a jack-of-all-trades can also increase your currency with start-ups who have ambitions to scale up and need devs who can cover both front-end and back-end languages and DevOps.

Time zones count

While tech companies are increasingly open to the idea of devs not being based in the same country, being in a different time zone is still a no-no. Few businesses can wait 12 hours for a critical problem to be solved. Many peripatetic devs choose to base themselves in Central or South America, to align with companies in the US, or in central Europe to stay in time with companies in the UK, France and Germany.

Basing yourself somewhere out of phase with your clients may make it harder to find work, and can mean working unsociable hours to fit in meetings and stand-ups and complete sprints on schedule, which may not be the carefree life you were looking for.

Build your client base

Get your client pool in place before heading off. Most companies will require agency or in-house experience before they'll hire you as a devs freelancer. You'll also need an online portfolio; if your employer has a non-disclosure agreement to prevent you sharing work created under contract, get involved in open-source projects where you can freely showcase your talents. A useful freelance devs starting point is to become a Code Mentor (www.codementor.io), reviewing code, debugging and providing tech advice for new coders. The website Arc (www.arc.dev) is another useful tool for finding freelance work. You'll also find listings on Remote (www.remote.co), Working Nomads (www.workingnomads.co/jobs), Just Remote (www.justremote.co) and Flexjobs (www.flexjobs.com).

CREATE A READY-TO-GO CONTRACT

When working for lots of smaller clients, it may be useful to draw up a standard contract that you can use for multiple projects with just small adjustments to match the work involved. Sample templates can be found online but make sure your contract covers the following:

★ **Expectations and responsibilities for both parties** What the work is, what is not covered, when work is due and what resources are provided.

★ **Intellectual Property Rights and Confidentiality** Spell out the client's right to confidentiality and ownership of intellectual property on completion of the work.

★ **The process for work reports** Agree the procedure for submitting reports on your progress, test results, etc.

★ **An Independent Contractor clause** Make it legally clear that you are providing services as an independent contractor to avoid tax issues.

★ **Legal protections** Make sure the contract spells out that you cannot be held responsible for future damages, or claims if the client breaches someone else's intellectual property in any materials provided to you.

★ **Terms of payment** Agree what is to be paid, when, and how, and clarify who is responsible for bank charges and currency conversions.

★ **Terms of termination** All contracts should specify the process should either party decide to terminate the agreement.

Market your talents

Nobody is going to hire you if they don't know about you, so use the full resources of the Web to market your skills and abilities. Starting an industry-specific blog can be a great place to broadcast your talents to the world, and you can use social media to drum up extra attention for your posts.

Ask clients for endorsements on LinkedIn and seek referrals to grow your network of possible clients. Don't forget to build your reputation as an expert (and grow your skills at the same time) by contributing and sharing your knowledge via developer communities such as Stack Overflow (www.stackoverflow.com), GitHub (www.github.com) and Dzone (www.dzone.com).

© MARC ROMANELLI / GETTY IMAGES

Consider full-time remote work

The software industry is increasingly open to offering full-time employment on remote contracts, though these roles are heavily in demand. To secure a location-independent full-time job, you'll be competing for work with a global pool of talent, so you'll need to be at the top of your game. The websites RemoteOK (www.remoteok.io) and WeWorkRemotely (www.weworkremotely.com) are good places to start your search.

Working the web

Huge numbers of web designers, web developers and SEO specialists galavant around the world while they work, sourcing new clients remotely as they go. Indeed, many website owners are completely unaware that their website was actually designed by someone working on the other side of the globe.

Designer or developer?

People who can build websites are always in demand, and it's comparatively easy to pick up the basic skills and learn as you go, building your experience with each new assignment. For web developers, the focus is on programming languages and behind-the-scenes apps; for web designers, it's all about the appearance of the finished website.

Clients have demands that may or may not be achievable, so you'll need good people skills and patience to make sure customers are happy with the end result. The first thing you'll need is your own beautifully designed website to show off everything you are capable of, and your portfolio of past projects. Dribbble (www.dribbble.com), Coroflot (www.coroflot.com) and Behance (www.behance.net) are good places to see what other designers are doing.

For the design side of the process, you'll need a suite of design applications on your laptop for processing and manipulating images – Creative Cloud from Adobe (www.adobe.com) is industry standard. You'll also need a library of fonts to give clients maximum customisability for their sites.

Get trained

If you're a newbie, it's worth getting training in writing HTML, coding in Cascading Style Sheets (CSS), and creating apps in Javascript and JQuery. Also look into User Experience (UX) and User Interface (UI) design; most clients are looking for a site that not only looks great but also provides a great experience for users. Popular online coding courses include SkillCrush (www.skillcrush.com), Codeacademy (www.codeacademy.com) and freeCodeCamp (www.freecodecamp.org).

SEO

Looking good is just part of the equation; to be seen, a website also needs great Search Engine Optimisation (SEO) to come top of the list of results in user searches. A whole industry has grown up advising businesses on the best ways to top the rankings, opening up lucrative opportunities for paid freelance work.

To start, sign up for some courses and workshops in SEO and internet marketing; The Beginner's Guide from Moz (https://moz.com/beginners-guide-to-seo) is a useful toe-in-the-water for understanding the basics. Check SEO Round Table (www.seroundtable.com) and Search Engine Land (www.searchengineland.com) for the latest news on changes to search engine algorithms.

© RAWIWANO / SHUTTERSTOCK

TOP TIP

'Part of the appeal of web development is that it's a portable skill. It's possible to teach yourself to code with online courses. Most big cities have coding bootcamps, which will have you job-ready in a few months. Some tech companies are fully remote and don't mind where you're based as long as you do a good job.'

Lucy Monie Hall, web developer and former Lonely Planet editor

Finding gigs

To find work, hone your skills and search freelance sites such as Upwork (www.upwork.com) and People Per Hour (www.peopleperhour.com). To break into SEO, contact potential clients, analysing their content and suggesting strategies for improvement, with results that can be measured by analytics.

Being virtually there

Once upon a time, providing business support meant being a physical shoulder to cry on – literally, in some cases. These days, all manner of services are provided remotely, from accounting and IT support to managing social media accounts.

Keep in time

The key criteria for most businesses is that the people providing support are in the same time zone as the business or its customers. Unless you fancy working through the night, providing tech support for companies in the US from a beach resort in Bali is probably not going to fly. Supporting Asian customers for a US company, on the other hand, could be just the work you are looking for.

Become a Virtual Assistant

A virtual assistant (VA) does everything a normal assistant does, but from somewhere else. Personal virtual assistants support individuals; executive virtual assistants provide support across the business. This could be secretarial work, office admin, diary management, invoicing, book-keeping – anything, really, that helps with the running of the business. Check out the Virtual Assistant Handbook (www.thevahandbook.com) for an overview.

Companies are more likely to hire you for specific tasks rather than as a general dogsbody, so experience counts. Find freelance jobs on sites such as Upwork (www.upwork.com) and Freelancer (www.freelancer.com) using combinations of 'virtual', 'assistant', 'help' or 'support' and terms associated with the industry you work in.

Managing social media

Managing social media accounts for private companies offers easy work for digitally-native digital nomads. The actual work could be anything from posting updates from the company Twitter account to forging alliances with influencers. As you'll be managing company accounts, work is best done via a Virtual Private Network (VPN).

As well as being a wizard with Twitter, Facebook, Instagram and other social platforms, it helps to have experience in marketing, SEO, public relations, or communications. This is a results-led industry, so you'll need to prove you are reaching the desired audience using tools such as Twitter Analytics (https://analytics.twitter.com), Facebook Audience Insights (www.facebook.com/ads/audience_insights) and Google Analytics (https://analytics.google.com).

Many people find their first role via LinkedIn, or through industry-specific groups and forums. Also search for gigs on freelance job sites, such as Upwork (www.upwork.com) and Freelancer (www.freelancer.com).

Tech support

With relevant tech skills, it's easy to find remote work providing tech support via online chat platforms, video streaming or digital voice calls. The key skills needed are a firm grasp of the technology you are supporting, strong computer literacy, and excellent communication skills.

Look for gigs that are directly relevant to your past experience, using your business network and industry-relevant search terms plus 'support' on remote working sites, such as Flexjobs (www.flexjobs.com), Freelancer (www.freelancer.com) and Upwork (www.upwork.com).

Online creativity

There are a hundred creative ways of making a living while you travel. Indeed, if you have any skill that doesn't require you to be stuck in a fixed location, this could be the foundation of a thriving digital nomad career.

Become a snapper

Travel photography is almost as popular as travel writing with digital nomads, and as a bonus, the same photograph can be sold under license multiple times to different clients. The downside is the cost of equipment – a quality DSLR camera and a set of fast lenses is the bare minimum, and you'll have the added expense of digital storage for memory-thirsty image files, and insurance to keep your kit in working order. You'll also need to invest in photo-editing software – Adobe Photoshop is the industry standard.

One often-missed money-making rule is to look for gaps in coverage. There are a million shots of the Taj Mahal, but comparatively few of bars in Delhi – fill the latter gap and you'll have much less competition if a client comes looking for Delhi nightlife shots. Always think about what image buyers may be looking for, and mix up obvious, eye-catching shots of sights with less obvious attractions, unstaged images of people doing things, and travel infrastructure.

Search the websites of stock agencies like Getty (www.gettyimages.co.uk), Alamy (www.alamy.com) and Shutterstock (www.shutterstock.com) to identify coverage gaps in your travel destinations. Agency websites will also explain how to get your images onto their site, so they can start earning money; photographer-friendly 500Px (web.500px.com) is one of the easiest options. And always highlight existing images and your availability for commissioned shoots on your website, Instagram and Twitter.

CORE KIT

The core piece of kit is subscription-based Adobe Creative Cloud (www.adobe.com/uk/creativecloud); the package includes industry-standard applications such as Photoshop (for image editing), Premiere Pro (for video), Illustrator (for graphics) and Adobe Portfolio (handy for creating a portfolio website).

Make movies

Websites always want video, but the glut of mobile phone clips means you'll only make money with professional-standard work. You'll need a sturdy tripod, external microphone and quality HD camera with optical rather than digital zoom; factor in Adobe Premiere Pro editing software, too. Always shoot close and from a distance, and zoom in on details using shallow depth of field to isolate subjects. Set the scene with establishing shots, narrow in on hands and faces during interviews, find ways to add movement to inanimate objects – clouds, traffic etc – and bring footage to life by filming people doing things. Build a portfolio, share footage on Twitter and Instagram, show your best work on your blog or website, and sell it through stock agencies such as Pond5 (www.pond5.com) and big-name Shutterstock or Adobe Stock.

Become a graphic designer

Graphic design is another extremely portable trade, though you might have to add a drawing tablet and stylus to your list of tech kit. Adobe Photoshop and Illustrator are essential pieces of software. You'll also need a way to store your work, either on external hard-drives or more safely on Google Drive (www.google.com/drive), Dropbox (www.dropbox.com) or another cloud-based server. Before you set off, develop your website as an online portfolio of work and share your creations widely on social media.

Begin the quest for graphic design gigs at freelance job sites such as 99 Designs (www.99designs.co.uk), Fiverr (www.fiverr.com), Upwork (www.upwork.com) and startup-oriented AngelList (www.angel.co). Many designers supplement their income by selling one-off designs on sites such as Creative Market (www.creativemarket.com) and Freepik (www.freepik.com).

Make beautiful music

Since music turned digital, producers and sound engineers have been able to edit and mix music from the road. To set up your laptop as a portable DAW (digital audio workstation), you'll need mountains of processing power and a pared-down recording kit with an audio interface, a portable audio recorder, monitor headphones and a USB midi-keyboard. Almost everything else, from virtual drum kits to vintage amps, can be added using digital plug-ins.

Primary income sources for audio nomads include making music for video games, instrumental backing tracks for advertising, and sample packs and loops for music producers. Music stock libraries, such as Audio Jungle (www.audiojungle.net) and Pond 5 (www.pond5.com), are good places to start selling work, or track down freelance sound jobs on freelance sites such as Upwork (www.upwork.com) and People Per Hour (www.peopleperhour.com).

© OZGUR DONMAZ / ISTOCK / GETTY IMAGES

TOP TIP

'Cloud-based storage is a must for any creative digital nomad. Google Drive gives you 15 GB of online storage for free, and you can upgrade for a fee, adding storage in 25 GB blocks. Otherwise, try Dropbox, with a free basic 2GB account, or 3TB of storage for US$10 per month.'

Joe Bindloss, travel writer, www.bindloss.co.uk

Distance learning made easy

Teaching English as a Foreign Language (TEFL; www.tefl.org) has been a mainstay for working travellers for decades, and many digital nomads supplement web-based work with stints at language schools. With a TEFL or TESOL (Teaching English to Speakers of Other Language; www.tesol.org) qualification you can teach almost anywhere.

Of course, traditional classroom teaching isn't particularly portable. The good news is that there is growing interest in online language teaching, particularly in China, using video-streaming tools to give remote lessons to school classrooms and one-to-one students.

Language teaching online

The entry requirements to work as an online language teacher are within grasp of most digital nomads. Language schools generally ask for a degree qualification in any subject and a TEFL or TESOL certificate, which you can study for online or locally at language schools in hundreds of locations around the world.

Most schools are focused on students in China and Korea and some programmes are limited to American and Canadian teachers. Qualifying teachers can find well-paid hourly work teaching classrooms via VipKid (https://t.vipkid.com.cn) and SayABC (https://t.sayabc.com), and similar work for slightly lower rates at Cambly (www.cambly.com), English Hunt (www.englishuntusa.com) and QKids (https://teacher.qkids.net).

It's also possible to find work providing one-to-one language teaching via mobile phone apps, such as NiceTalk (http://tutor.nicetalk.com), Palfish (www.ipalfish.com) and Tandem (www.tandem.net), reducing your baggage allowance even further.

Lost in translation

Polyglots can find lucrative work translating written text. Exactly what you do will depend on the languages you speak, but being able to translate, for example, Japanese into Arabic will make you particularly in demand. Find gigs via sites such as Upwork (www.upwork.com), Freelancer (www.freelancer.com) and ProZ (www.proz.com). Translate (www.translate.com/translators), One Hour Translation (www.onehourtranslation.com) and UnBabel (www.unbabel.com) also have paid openings for online translators.

© HERO IMAGES / GETTY IMAGES

Other kinds of teaching

Thanks to the wonder of video streaming, you can teach almost anything remotely, from playing guitar to using WordPress or mastering SEO. All you need is a fast connection, a webcam (or two) and a structured approach to learning that makes students feel they are getting value for their buck. To find students, you'll need to advertise your services, through your own website or blog, via social media, or through more conventional advertising channels. Many online teachers offer free sweetener lessons on YouTube (www.youtube.com) to tempt users to subscribe to paid lessons.

WHERE TO GO

Choosing a destination

Okay, you've done the hard part and decided to go. The next big question is where to begin? Most digital nomads move to new locations several times a year, usually to fit around visa restrictions or to avoid hot summers and cold winters, but the journey has to start somewhere. Short of sticking a pin in a map, what is the best way to choose your first base as a freshly initiated digital nomad? Here are some ideas.

Start small

Don't be too ambitious with your first destination. Look for somewhere with solid infrastructure, low living costs, loads of co-working spaces, and a comfortable quality of life that won't take too much adjusting to get used to. If you already speak the language, even better. Countries that grant a long, visa-free stay on arrival are always a good bet; leave visa-runs and freelancer visas until you have decided the nomad lifestyle is definitely for you. There'll be plenty of time later for exploring those emerging, off-the-map locations.

Work hard, play hard

Make your first hub somewhere you can enjoy yourself as well as work. For most nomads, travel is at least as important as work, so pick somewhere you've always wanted to visit, with lots of exciting things to do in the local area. Your living costs are likely to be higher at the start of a trip than they are once you know the ropes, and free things to do like surfing, hiking and exploring new neighbourhoods will mean fewer worries about balancing your budget. Whatever else you do, don't blow your emergency fund on two weeks of sky-diving at the start of your trip!

Be a social nomad

On your first couple of stops, you'll be a rookie, so there's no harm approaching the older cops on the force. Pick a hub with a well-developed nomad scene, and a busy calendar of networking and social events for remote workers. As a general rule, the bigger the pool of co-working spaces, the greater the opportunities to connect with other nomads for tips and support.

Ask a nomad

Not every destination will be a perfect fit. If you're unsure about a nomad hub, ask remote workers who are already there for an honest appraisal. Chris the Freelancer (www.christhefreelancer.com) is just one of a growing contingent of digital nomads posting destination reports as they travel from hub to hub. Join local Facebook groups for nomads and expats and ask around to get the lowdown from people already living in the destination.

Make a first-year plan

All being well, stop number one will be such a success that you'll want to keep on going, so make a plan for how long you'll stay in your first hub and where you'll move to after. Consider the costs of travel and the seasons; plenty of nomads let the climate dictate when they go next, taking advantage of the best weather in each location. Picking a hub with easy links to neighbouring countries is a sensible step. In areas such as Eastern Europe and Southeast Asia, it's possible to find a new digital hub just by crossing the nearest border.

Be ready for change

One surefire route to a stressful trip is to impose too many conditions before you arrive. Do have a wireframe plan, but be prepared to change it up once you arrive. Being a digital nomad offers a level of freedom you may never have again – don't hold yourself back by being too tied to a set itinerary.

TOP TIP

'Originally, when I started travelling, I'd move to a new location once a week. Eventually I slowed down and started staying 3 months in any one location. My favourite places to travel are Eastern Europe in the summer (low cost of living, good internet, great nightlife), moving to Southeast Asia when its gets cold. Winter is optional.' **Piotr Gryko, remote software developer, www.piotrgryko.com**

Be business smart

Fun is important but never forget the work side of the equation. This is your full-time job, so be disciplined from the start about when you need to work and when you're free to relax. Choose a destination with fast internet speeds and the necessary infrastructure to support your business, and consider time zones – if your clients are in North America and you're in Taipei, 12 hours ahead of EDT, all your meetings will be first thing in the morning or last thing at night.

© TAKE PHOTO / SHUTTERSTOCK

FIVE VITAL ATTRIBUTES FOR A DIGITAL DESTINATION

© 2020, DOJO BALI

There are digital nomad hubs across the globe, from high-tech megacities to medieval country towns and laid-back beach resorts. But all share a few key elements in common. Here are the key attributes for a digital nomad destination.

Highly connected

As a location-independent professional, the most important thing you need to keep your business thriving is fast internet access. How fast will depend on the nature of the work you are doing – bloggers, photographers and other nomads who can take their work offline may be fine using public wi-fi connections with download speeds as low as 5 Mbps. IT professionals may need speeds of 100 Mbps or higher, which usually means working from paid-for co-working spaces.

Cafes, co-working & community

As a footloose remote worker, having somewhere to work is pretty essential. Some digital nomads work entirely from coffee shops with free wi-fi, reducing workspace costs to a couple of cappuccinos per day, while others look for high-tech work spaces where they can network with other location-independent professionals in a more conventional office environment. Look for cities with plenty of both, and well-established Facebook groups, meetups and social events for digital nomads that new arrivals can plug into.

Easy visas

A digital hub where you can only get a visa for a two-week stay is no good to anyone. The best nomad destinations offer inexpensive visas or visa-free travel lasting several months, so you can settle down for good stint of work before you have to worry about moving on or renewing your papers. Some destinations make special concessions to entice digital nomads – Tbilisi in Georgia offers visa-free travel for a year, while Tallinn in Estonia has special visa categories for digital nomads.

Abundant accommodation

If you plan to stay somewhere for a long time, it's essential that you can find a room or flat to rent without having to join a queue. Even hostels can get expensive if you are staying for several months, and after the first couple of weeks, almost everyone craves their own space to work in. Look for hub cities with lots of rooms and apartments for rent, and turn to other nomads for advice on finding a place to stay.

Low-cost living

Many people make good livings as digital nomads, but the lifestyle is centred on cities with low living costs. Look for cities with inexpensive food and accommodation, free public wi-fi, cost-effective co-working spaces and low-cost public transport. Note that most nomad hubs are cheaper than home, rather than being arbitrarily cheap; staying anywhere for a long period of time brings lots of costs and there are few places where you can live comfortably as a digital nomad for less than US$1000 per month.

TYPES OF DIGITAL HUBS

Digital hubs come in all shapes and sizes, from chilled-out surf resorts to Asian megacities. Most fit into one of the following categories.

THE TECH METROPOLIS

Some of the best hubs for digital nomads are vibrant, modern cities – often in Asia – with young populations, cutting-edge tech industries and well-established networks of local entrepreneurs. In these space-age hubs, co-working spaces are as likely to be filled with local devs as out-of-towners, and the opportunities to set up new business partnerships are boundless. The flip side is that living costs are higher than average, and there's heavy competition for accommodation.

THE EMERGING CAPITAL

Europe is dotted with small countries that are emerging as dynamic places to do business, away from the red tape of the big European powers. Historic capitals such as Tbilisi, Budapest and Tallinn serve up a perfect platter of low living costs, tech-friendly infrastructure, and a can-do attitude to trying new things. Typical characteristics of these hubs include easy visa regulations, innovative co-working spaces and centuries of history, but more focus on work than play, which will appeal to some nomads more than others.

THE SECOND CITY

Across the world, so-called 'primate' cities are hoovering up the bulk of the tech talent, offering endless opportunities to those who can manage the stratospheric living costs. Enter the second cities – typically the second-largest in the country – where local politicians are pulling out the stops to make things easy for business, the cost of living is manageable, and competition for space and resources is that little bit less cutthroat. These kinds of hubs offer a gentler experience, and the chance to feel like a local while you remote-work for clients on the other side of the globe.

THE BACKPACKER HANGOUT

THE WORK– HARD, PLAY– HARD RESORT

Many of Asia's best loved digital hubs started out as old-fashioned backpacker hangouts, before travellers with laptops kick-started the co-working movement. These kinds of hubs offer loads of activities, cheap food, oodles of short-term accommodation and intense nightlife, but can be lacking in local atmosphere. These are also easy places to burn through money. Some love the scene, others want to feel more involved in the country they are working in.

Digital nomads love hobbies, and there are plenty of digital hubs in beach resorts known for surfing and other wet-and-wild activities. Few nomads actually work on the beach – for one thing, it's hard to see the screen – but easy access to sand and surf at the end of a working day has obvious appeal. Resort hubs tend to be smaller, with fewer co-working spaces and slower internet, but plenty to do after hours. Most do get mobbed by tourists at certain times of year, pushing up prices in peak season.

© WESTEND61 / GETTY IMAGES

TOP TIP

'As a digital nomad you are in a privileged position – you can choose to work almost anywhere in the world. Pick a city that appeals to you culturally, where there are things you want to do, where you are in love with the food and the way of life. This is at least as important as the number of co-working spaces.'

Joe Bindloss, travel writer, www.bindloss.co.uk

© OLEKSIY MARK / SHUTTERSTOCK

Getting there

Digital nomads have more flexibility than most when it comes to booking flights, trains, buses and ferries. Not only can you travel at any time, you can travel anywhere, and change your travel plans on impulse if a new opportunity arises. This puts nomads in a great position to pick up cheap deals.

© OLESYA KUZNETSOVA / SHUTTERSTOCK

© KELLY CHENG TRAVEL PHOTOGRAPHY / GETTY IMAGES

 BE FLEXIBLE

As the master of your own destiny, you can travel when you want, where you want. Plan your travel to avoid heavily subscribed routes and peak times like school holidays, and you'll save significantly. This even applies at a weekly level – many business travellers fly out on Monday and back on Friday, while weekend breakers fly out on Fridays, back on Sundays, so prices often dip on less popular days such as Saturday, Tuesday and Wednesday.

 MONITOR THE AIRWAYS

Flight prices fluctuate constantly, so book when they hit rock bottom. Visit fare-tracking sites like Skiplagged (www.skiplagged.com), TravelZoo (www.travelzoo.com), Travel Pirates (www.travelpirates.com) and The Flight Deal (www.theflightdeal.com). The sweet spot for cheap fares is typically between two and one and a half months before travel. Kayak (www.kayak.co.uk) includes a price forecast in search results; Skyscanner (www.skyscanner.net) has a useful map search which shows starting prices to cities worldwide for any particular hub.

LOOK OUT FOR AIRLINE DEALS

When airlines offer new routes, prices are often discounted to lure in customers, particularly for long haul, so signing up to email newsletters from airlines is a great way to spot upcoming bargains. Skyscanner (www.skyscanner.net) also posts regular updates on lower-than-average fares. Don't overlook error fares; even airlines make mistakes and flights are sometimes mistakenly offered for less than the going rate, so watch for notifications in email newsletters and social media posts from discount flight sites.

 ## USE ALTERNATIVE AIRPORTS

Many travellers pay over the odds to get to their chosen city when flying to a smaller airport nearby would be cheaper. As a digital nomad, you have the flexibility to fly to the country next door and take a train across the border, or jump on a bus from an airport close to your final destination. Flights to Penang in Malaysia, for example, are more expensive than flying into Kuala Lumpur and zipping to Georgetown on the train or bus, while budget flights to Asia from Avalon Airport in Geelong can be half the price of flights from nearby Melbourne Tullamarine.

 ## GO HALFWAY ON BUDGET AIRLINES

Fares out of busy airports such as London Heathrow can be significantly lower than long haul trips from smaller European hubs, so a short trip to a major hub on a budget airline can save hundreds of dollars on the total cost of a long distance trip. This usually means booking the trip on two separate tickets – if you miss your long-haul flight because the budget flight was delayed, you won't get compensation, so allow a healthy time buffer between the two flights.

 ## USE YOUR AIR MILES

Most airlines offer frequent flier packages, and by sticking to particular airlines or alliances, you can quickly earn enough air miles for short-haul flights. The big three airline alliances are Star Alliance (www.staralliance.com), OneWorld (www.oneworld.com), and SkyTeam (www.skyteam.com); miles earned on one member can be redeemed with any airline in the same group. To maximise returns, consider paying all your business costs with a credit card linked to an air miles scheme, but be sure to clear the card debts every month to avoid high interest rates.

Alternative travel tips for environmentalists

In today's enlightened times, people are much more aware of the environmental effect of flying across the globe. The good news is you don't need to fly impulsively from hub to hub to have a fulfilling digital nomad life. Here are some tips for ways to reduce your carbon footprint when you travel.

Travel overland

As a digital nomad, the one thing you are not short of is time, so why rush to the next destination by air when you can take the scenic route? You'll have a much more memorable travel experience if you travel by bus or train, or even by electric car, plotting a route via useful digital hubs along the way. Base yourself in Southeast Asia, Central and South America or Europe and you can hop from country to country without ever having to go near an airport check-in desk. Check in with The Man in Seat 61 (www.seat61.com) for advice on international train travel.

© IMAGE SOURCE / GARY JOHN NORMAN / GETTY IMAGES

© PETE SEAWARD / LONELY PLANET

Go by boat

Sixteen-year-old Greta Thunberg travelled by boat from England to New York for the UN Climate Action Summit in 2019, so there should be nothing stopping you travelling to your next hub by boat or ferry. However, different boats have different footprints – large ocean-going cruisers produce more carbon per passenger than planes, while sailing boats have almost no operating carbon-footprint at all. Obviously, travelling by sea takes longer than flying, but ferries are the default mode of transport between many island nations. Search on Ferrylines (www.ferrylines.com) to find international routes worldwide.

Seek out sustainable co-working spaces

Many co-working spaces are turning green, reducing their energy use and recycling and composting to reduce waste. Measures taken can be as subtle as reusing coffee grounds as fertiliser or as big-picture as running the whole office using renewable energy. The data centres that power the internet have a similar carbon footprint to the aviation industry, so reducing your energy use while you surf is definitely a step forward. Most co-working spaces are up front about their environmental policies, so ask for details before you join.

TOP TIP

'The electric vehicle (EV) industry is booming, making environmentally friendly long-distance travel easier than ever. Plug-in networks are particularly extensive in Western Europe, North America, Japan and China, but just watch as the world catches up. If you can't find a rental company offering EVs, try contacting peer-to-peer schemes and car clubs in the area.'

Dora Ball, travel editor, @dorawhit

OFFSET YOUR TRAVELS

Reducing your carbon footprint should be the primary objective, but for the carbon you can't avoid, consider joining a carbon-offsetting programme, where you contribute financially to green projects to compensate for the carbon created by flying. It's not a perfect system – some schemes have been accused of being a licence to pollute so wealthy travellers can feel less guilty as they flit around the globe – so seek out offsetting activities that have been certified under the Gold Standard (www.goldstandard.org), Climate Action Reserve (www.climateactionreserve.org), Plan Vivo (www.planvivo.org) or Verra (www.verra.org) schemes, for more confidence that your money is making a difference.

BEFORE YOU GO

Pre-departure health essentials

The most important factor in staying healthy on the road is making sure you're healthy before you leave. Take regular exercise, eat a balanced diet, don't smoke, and drink alcohol in moderation. Visit your doctor for a pre-trip checkup, and to confirm any vaccinations that might be needed for your destinations. Check in with Travel Health Pro (www.travelhealthpro.org.uk) for pre-departure insights.

Visit your doctor for a general check-up

If there's anything amiss, it's better to know before you go. If you have a known health complaint, bring your prescription, with the generic as well as the branded names for any drugs, and any other important medical paperwork. If you have allergies, make sure you have any necessary medication, and carry flashcards with an explanation of your condition and treatment in the local language.

Don't forget your eyes & teeth!

Go to the dentist, and visit your optician for an up-to-date glasses prescription and a general eye health check. Buying glasses and having dental work can be much cheaper abroad than at home, but it's better to have everything checked first by a trusted professional. If you wear contact lenses, order an extra supply, and carry extra lens fluid (open bottles do not last as long in the heat).

Get your jabs

A month or so ahead of travel, get any vaccinations you need for your trip. Specialist travel clinics will have vaccinations for most common illnesses in stock, but prices can be higher than if you visit your normal doctor. It may take several weeks to gain immunity after a vaccination, so don't leave things till the last minute. Many courses of anti-malarial tablets also need to start before you leave.

Carrying meds

If you have an existing health condition, make sure you have enough medication, and know the generic, non-branded name for your meds in case you need to find them in another country. Bring more than you need and split your supply so it doesn't all go missing if you lose a piece of luggage. Note that some countries ban the import of specific medications – for example, Japan bans medicines containing the painkiller codeine and the decongestant Pseudoephedrine.

Get insured

On any trip, travel insurance with comprehensive health cover is essential. Look for a policy that includes evacuation in the event of a medical emergency, and find out if the policy pays hospitals directly, or whether you need to pay upfront yourself and claim back later. Some countries have reciprocal health care agreements with your home country, but you'll usually need a card to prove eligibility – again, look into this before you go.

Money & budgeting

Making the decision to go is the first step to a new life as a digital nomad, but you won't get far on good intentions alone. Becoming a location-independent worker costs money, particularly at the start of the journey. You'll need to budget for flights, visas, travel insurance and day-to-day living in a new city, plus additional costs for running your business. You'll also need an emergency fund, to cover you for the times you can't work or gaps between projects, and to help you get home if you decide to bail on the nomadic life.

Zero out your debts

Digital nomads with debts tend not to be digital nomads for long. Before you go, try to clear any outstanding money you owe. The goal is, remember, to have all your money fully available to fund a life of travel. If you have a mortgage and intend to keep your house or apartment, rent it out to cover the monthly payments and appoint a management company to deal with all the admin. Look for landlord insurance packages that include a guaranteed rent for any periods when you can't find a tenant.

Build up a nest egg

Before you say sayonara to your old life, you'll need to build up a cushion of money to fund your start-up costs and cover you for emergencies while you build up your remote-working business. Having an emergency stash of cash to pay for replacing your laptop if it is lost or stolen is pretty much essential. Put on your accountant's visor and work out exactly how much you need to get to your first destination and live for two months with no income at all, then add 50% as a buffer in case of headwinds.

Know your limits

Set yourself a minimum level your savings can drop to before alarm klaxons sound. If things go south

and you need to pull the emergency chute, having enough money to clear outstanding costs in the destination, fly home, and fund yourself while you slot back into normal life will help you avoid more stress than you can put a price on.

BUDGET CHECKLIST

Do you have enough money to...?

When building up and maintaining your emergency fund, aim for enough money to cover the following for at least two months:

★ Eating and accommodation costs
★ Your internet access
★ Your mobile phone bill
★ Co-working space membership
★ Transport to where you work
★ Funds to replace your phone or laptop
★ Money for medical bills in an emergency
★ Cash for a flight home
★ Living costs while you find a job back home

TOP TIP

'When you first start travelling, it's all about experiences and it's easy to justify spending money. But when you do it for a living, you have to manage your cash-flow like any other business. Always maintain a decent emergency fund. If your only buffer is enough money for a flight home, those first few months will be the comedown of all comedowns after the no-ties life you've grown accustomed to.'

Joe Bindloss, travel writer, www.bindloss.co.uk

Managing your money overseas

However you choose to get paid, you'll need a safe and secure way to manage your money overseas. Most nomads get paid to an account that they can access over the internet, but for real-life day-to-day living costs, you need to be able to access your cash, often in hard currency. If clients are paying into an account that charges you high fees for each overseas card payment or ATM withdrawal, a chunk of your hard-earned cash will be keeping bankers in champers, rather than supporting your digital nomad lifestyle.

Carrying cash

No matter how much your destination has moved towards a cashless economy, you'll need access to hard currency for small costs such as coffees, snacks and public transport. The golden rule when withdrawing cash from an ATM overseas is to make larger withdrawals less often, to avoid repeated bank charges. Keep your hard currency safe in a money pouch worn against the skin, rather than a pickpocket-friendly wallet carried in the easy-to-access back pocket of your jeans.

An emergency stash

Store a supply of cash in US dollars, UK pounds or Euros hidden somewhere safe as a last-ditch emergency fund, in case you don't have access to your accounts (think power cuts, communication blackouts, political unrest). Travellers cheques also work for this purpose, and have the added advantage that they can be replaced if they get lost or stolen, but they are falling from favour with travellers and are accepted by fewer and fewer outlets.

© 2020, KAPTAR, BUDAPEST

Pay by phone

Paying by phone is taking the world by storm, including in many developing nations. Apps such as Apple Pay (www.apple.com/uk/apple-pay) and Google Pay (https://pay.google.com) function as digital wallets, allowing users to make contactless payments using the NFC (Near-field Communication) chip inside the phone. To use the apps, you'll need to load details of your debit and credit cards, but there are no additional fees on top of what the card issuers charge (the app company charges a small fee to the card issuer but this doesn't come from your end). The downside? Mobile payment only works at places that are set up for contactless payments.

Plastic fantastic

The default way to pay for many travellers, credit and debit cards are easy to use and simple to cancel if lost or stolen. But pre-advise your bank if travelling to a fraud-heavy destination to prevent your card being blocked, and monitor statements regularly in case of card cloning. Also consider bringing a 'clean' backup credit card (with no payments outstanding).

Using a prepaid debit card avoids transaction fees and punitive exchange rates; top it up from whichever account clients are paying into. Caxton FX (www.caxtonfx.com), Revolut (www.revolut.com) and FairFX (www.fairfx.com) are major prepaid players, but shop around in your home country, too. Where possible, make card payments in local currency to avoid the poor exchange rates offered by retailers.

© 2020, DOJO BALI

HANDY MONEY APPS

★ **XE (www.xe.com)** The world's most popular currency exchange app offers real-time exchange rates between every global currency, and stores the last-checked rates for your 10 favourite currencies for times when you can't get online.

★ **Trabee Pocket (www.trabeepocket.com)** A handy travel expenses tracker that can help you keep on top of incomings and outgoings, and split your costs into different categories – handy for spotting if your beer budget is pushing you over the limit.

★ **Splittr (www.splittr.io)** Designed for groups of travellers sharing costs and splitting bills, Splittr also works as a tool for monitoring your own non-business travel costs.

★ **WeSwap (www.weswap.com)** Combining an app and a pre-paid card, WeSwap uses peer-to-peer transfers to cut out the costs of going through normal foreign exchange channels. There are 18 supported currencies, exchange fees are modest, and exchange rates are better than on the high street – but you'll need to wait seven days to access your money, or pay a fee.

★ **Starling (www.starlingbank.com)** Halfway between a bank account and a pre-paid debit card, this UK-based mobile-only bank charges no fees for overseas ATM withdrawals and card transactions made with the contactless Mastercard that comes with each account.

Getting paid

As a location-independent freelancer, you'll need to give some thought to how you get paid. Bank accounts tend to be designated in a particular currency and operate in a particular jurisdiction, under a particular tax regime. Whenever money moves between banks, countries or currencies, there are fees to pay, and you'll be hostage to the bank's foreign exchange rates, which usually benefit the bank rather than the recipient.

Deciding who will pay these fees and charges adds an extra layer of complication to fee negotiations with international clients. Most freelancers grudgingly swallow the bank charges to avoid alienating clients with complicated payment procedures, instead negotiating a fee that accounts for losing some of the lump sum in costs and charges. There are however other ways to get paid, though none are completely cost free; consider the following.

WORKING

© 2020, CAFE FLOR, BUENOS AIRES / PH. LARA JUSTET

Getting paid into a bank account
Opening a local bank account may not be an option for non-resident nomads; it's easier to have clients transfer payments via the SWIFT network, though you will pay charges for international transfers, and lose out on the exchange if your payment is in a different currency to your home bank account.

Paypal
On the face of things, Paypal (www.paypal.com) seems like a perfect solution for digital nomads. Clients can pay in from anywhere, you don't need to be based in any particular country, and you can transfer funds out digitally wherever you are in the world. However, Paypal payments incur a steep fee, typically 2.9% of the transfer amount plus a nominal service charge (this is how Paypal has managed to grow into such a massively profitable company). And this rises to 3.9% if the client account and your account are registered in different countries.

Paypal also uses its own internal foreign exchange rates every time money changes from one currency to another, eating a little more out of the transfer amount. Some nomads report being able to reduce fees using a Paypal Business account and invoicing using software that supports PayPal Business Payments, but this option isn't available to everyone.

© 2020, DOJO BALI

Digital currencies

We can't say we recommend using something as volatile as BitCoin to receive your payments, but some nomads do. Notwithstanding the environmental issues (mining cryptocurrencies burns through huge amounts of energy) the value of currencies such as BitCoin, Litecoin and Ethereum/Ether can fluctuate widely, making this more like speculation than banking. If you are not already a cryptocurrency holder, there are easier and safer ways to get paid.

Wire transfers

There are dozens of companies offering international wire transfers, and you can collect your money through a bank account, or in cash at one of their offices. However, they usually take a hefty cut, some of which may be hidden behind disadvantageous exchange rates. Western Union (www.westernunion.com) and Moneygram (www.moneygram.com) have offices worldwide, but for payments to bank accounts, you may lose less of your hard-earned lucre if clients send via an online-only wire transfer company such as Azimo (www.azimo.com) or OFX (www.ofx.com).

Transferwise

Online transfer company Transferwise (www.transferwise.com) reduces some of the costs of transferring money by maintaining its own reserve bank accounts in different countries. When money is transferred, the inbound payment goes into one account, and the outbound payment is made from another account, so no money actually moves across borders. There are still fees – starting from 0.35% of the transfer amount – but clients can make the transfer quickly online using a bank account or bank card, making this an easy and low-cost option for clients and freelancers.

Getting paid on time

One of the most important skills for any freelancer is staying on top of payments and invoices. Payment within 30 days is the accepted norm, but many clients take much longer, and need repeated reminding to actually send payments. Managing your books and making sure invoices are sent promptly and payments are received on time is as important to your business as doing the actual work – digital accounting software, such as Harvest (www.getharvest.com), Freshbooks (www.freshbooks.com) and Quickbooks (https://quickbooks.intuit.com) can help.

Invoice terms

Always specify the payment terms on your invoice – including that payment is due within 30 days of the date the invoice is issued, or less if appropriate. For industries where late payment fees are standard, also mention incremental interest fees that become due for each week that payment is delayed. Use digital accounting software to set reminders when payments are due, so you know when to send reminders to tardy clients.

Tax tips

Death is one thing you can't avoid, but things are more flexible when it comes to taxes, despite what people say. If you will be away from your home country for a large part of the year, you may be able to declare yourself non-resident for tax purposes, avoiding some of your tax obligations in your home country. The Worldwide Personal Tax and Immigration guide from Ernst & Young (search on www.ey.com) is a handy starting point for understanding the tax system in each country.

Personal versus corporation tax

It's important to know the difference between personal taxes (paid by individuals on earnings, in their resident country) and corporation taxes (paid by businesses on profits, after operating costs, in the country where the business is registered). It's possible to pay personal tax in one country, under one set of rules, and corporation tax in another under different rules. Some digital nomads avoid tax completely by becoming non-resident at home, and moving around to avoid being a resident of anywhere. This is a legal grey area, and you may not be comfortable dodging the taxes that pay for public services. But most nomads pay tax at home, or in countries where they'e temporarily resident – if only to avoid difficult questions from the tax officer if they eventually do return home.

Becoming non-resident

To qualify as non-resident, most countries require you to be overseas for significant periods – from 183 days to 349 days in any given year (check your home country's laws). Make the first move to notify the tax authorities, as making your status official will make it easier to reintegrate if you return home to work in future.

Become a tax exile

It's ethically iffy, but some high earners sidestep tax by becoming legally resident in another country with a low-tax (or tax-free) regime. Some tax havens offer temporary residency for a fee; others have residency schemes where you're not taxed on money earned outside the country. You'll need an accountant with offshore expertise.

© AMNARTK / SHUTTERSTOCK

© 2020, DOJO BALI

Setting up a company

As companies and employees are taxed separately, you can reduce your tax bill by setting up a company and paying yourself a salary (or dividend) through it. Your business will be liable for corporation tax, but only on profits after running costs. Your wage or dividends are liable for tax at personal (or dividend) rates, but earnings may be tax free if they fall below a certain threshold. The alternative is to set up as a sole trader (self-employed). You'll only pay tax on profits, and the business running costs are tax deductible, but company and personal finances are intertwined – you're personally liable if your business falls into debt or goes bust.

To set up a company, you'll normally have to officially register its name and submit annual accounts. Under Estonia's E-Residency scheme (www.e-resident.gov.ee), non-residents can register a business, with an associated local bank account, and only pay corporate tax on profits that are distributed as dividends.

TOP TIP

'As an individual (unless you are a US citizen), you'll pay tax in any country where you spend more than 183 days a year, but you can use that information for your benefit by becoming a permanent traveller. For your company, find a safe harbour that understands that you're a traveller.'

Ignacio Carvajal, digital entrepreneur and director, www.micropreneur.life

Paying taxes on the road

As a sole trader (ie a self-employed person) or employee of your own company, you'll be liable for personal income tax in the country where you are legally resident. However, if you are not resident anywhere, you may not be liable for personal income tax anywhere. Even if you become legally resident in a particular country, you may be able to avoid paying tax on income earned outside the country if you stay for less than 183 days.

However, the tax authorities in some countries are particularly efficacious at following citizens across borders. US residents, for example, are liable for some government taxes wherever they are in the world, for as long as they hold a US passport, subject to some complex exclusions.

Keeping your books

Whatever your approach to taxation, you'll need to keep track of your invoices, payments and costs. It's the best way to stay on top of your incomings and outgoings and you'll definitely need this information to file a tax return for your business. Hiring an accountant can take some of the pain out of the process.

If you're happy to cover the admin yourself, digital accounting packages such as Freshbooks (www.freshbooks.com), Harvest (www.getharvest.com) and Quickbooks (https://quickbooks.intuit.com) are well set up for tracking costs and invoices, and you can back up scans of your receipts to a cloud-based archive such as Evernote (www.evernote.com) so they're ready to hand when you file your annual accounts.

Visas & paperwork

The traditional digital nomad model is based on something of a legal loophole. Most governments have strict rules governing who can visit and work in the country, but the vast majority of nomadic remote workers travel on tourist visas, bypassing the normal rules and regulations for working in a foreign country.

 ## WORKING ON A TOURIST VISA

In theory, tourist visas are for holidays only, and anyone working overseas needs a business or work visa. If you were caught working for a local company on a tourist visa, the penalties would be severe. However, most digital nomads work for companies outside the country they are visiting, so the authorities are unlikely to be aware of your business activities unless you draw attention to yourself.

What this does mean is that most digital nomads are operating in a grey area of the law. Immigration rules are generally set up to protect local workers and make sure that visiting workers from elsewhere pay their taxes, and if the authorities discover you flouting the rules, you could be deported and blacklisted. On the other hand, the risks of anyone noticing that you are working are small, unless you become legally resident, in which case you'll become liable for local taxes like other residents.

 ## TOURIST VISA CONDITIONS

Most tourist visas are set up to make it as easy as possible for travellers to visit, so there are usually few restrictions. Many countries offer visas on arrival, often for free, and some offer visa-free travel for tourists. One condition most countries insist on is six months' validity in your passport beyond the date of entry; if your passport is close to expiry, get a new one before you set off. The website Visa List (www.visalist.io) details which countries require a visa; for specifics, contact the embassy of the country you're going to.

 ## ONWARD TICKETS

Another thing border officials may ask to see is an onward ticket, as proof you intend to leave the country at the end of your stay. Some people travel on return plane tickets, but never use the return leg. Others buy a cheap plane or ferry ticket to the nearest onward destination, and then cancel it for a refund once they have entered the country; the US site for Expedia (www.expedia.com) allows free cancellation within 24 hours.

Making fake tickets in Photoshop (believe us – people do it) is not recommended, and the same goes for websites that promise to knock up a convincing fake ticket, but sites such as Best Onward Ticket (www.bestonwardticket.com) and One Way Fly (www.onewayfly.com) let you 'rent' a ticket from travel agencies for a short period, proving that where there's a will, there's a way.

Work-friendly visas

Not every country requires you to have a visa to work legally. Citizens of the EU, or of a country in the European Economic Area, can move to other countries in the zone and work with few restrictions, though may need to register with the local authorities and obtain legal resident status if staying more than six months. Specialist visas for digital nomads, which allow work for short periods of time, remove all of this uncertainty.

Australian Working Holiday

https://immi.homeaffairs.gov.au/visas/getting-a-visa/visa-listing/work-holiday-417

The Australian Working Holiday scheme allows 18 to 30-year-olds to work for a year in the country without restrictions, including for local companies – or two years, if you're willing to spend three months working for a company in rural Australia. French, Irish and Canadian citizens can join the programme up to the age of 35 and you can extend for a third year if you do six months of rural work in year two. While not aimed at digital nomads, it certainly opens up Australia as a potential base for stints of work while travelling around Asia.

© 2020, THE HOUSE, LAS PALMAS

© 2020, PUNSPACE, CHIANG MAI

Thailand's Hand-to-Hand Combat Visa

www.mfa.go.th/main/en/services

Thousands of digital nomads work in Thailand on tourist visas, but this only allows a short stay of three to six months. To stay for a whole year, one option is to sign up for a year of training at a Chiang Mai *muay thai* (Thai boxing) academy. This can involve as little as four hours' training per week, and it removes the need for visa runs to neighbouring countries, but there's a THB 35,000 (US$1135) fee, on top of the costs of the course.

Rentista Visas for Costa Rica

www.migracion.go.cr/Paginas/Visas

The Costa Rican government has a special visa category for visitors who can prove they have a monthly income of US$2500 for a period of two years. Visa holders can work independently and even set up a local business, but they are not permitted to work as an employee for a Costa Rican company. The one complication is that the authorities may ask to see proof of funds to support yourself in the form of savings.

Mexico Residente Temporal Visa

www.gob.mx/tramites/ficha/visa-de-residencia-temporal/SRE260

The Residente Temporal Visa allows foreign citizens to upgrade the normal entry permit to a year-long, multiple-entry visa. You can work for clients overseas, but not Mexican companies, and can extend for up to four years. To qualify, you must be able to demonstrate a steady monthly income (from US$1600 to US$2500, depending on where you apply) for at least six months, and attend a pre-travel interview at a Mexican embassy overseas before you travel.

Germany Freiberufler (Freelancer) and Selbständiger (Self-Employed) Visas

https://service.berlin.de/dienstleistung/305249/en

Freelancers or self-employed people working in Germany for German clients can qualify for special work-enabled visas. The perk for many non-EU citizens is that you can enter Germany visa-free as a tourist, then apply later at the local Ausländerbehörde (Foreigner's Office). There are conditions, including a fixed address in Germany and working in one of the long list of approved freelance industries.

Estonia Digital Nomad Visa

Estonia has announced plans for a new Digital Nomad Visa, allowing location-independent professionals to work in the country for up to a year, with the added bonus of visa-free travel within the Schengen Area. This could be the perfect time to set up base in the country described by Wired magazine as the most advanced digital society in the world. Estonia also runs an e-Residency scheme (www.e-resident.gov.ee), allowing entrepreneurs to set up online businesses here remotely, and a special visa for owners of start-ups (www.startupestonia.ee).

THE VISA RUN

Travelling on a standard tourist visa can cause problems for digital nomads. Most are valid for between one and three months and, officially, should not be used for working while in the country. Similar rules apply to visa-free entry, for which you may have to show evidence of enough money to support yourself during your stay, or an onward plane ticket – all of which stands in the way of the fancy-free lifestyle you were signing up for.

Crossing the border

The good news is that many countries popular with digital nomads do not mind how long you leave the country for at the end of your stay, so long as you physically cross the border. Many nomads get into a regular routine of making the so-called visa run every couple of months, flying or crossing overland to a neighbouring country before re-entering on a brand new tourist visa.

Historically, the authorities have turned a blind eye to this rather obvious piece of bending the rules, but with the volume of nomads zipping back and forth across borders in destinations such as Thailand, immigration officials are becoming less accepting of travellers making repeated entries and exits via the same border crossing.

To avoid getting locked out of your chosen digital hub with bills still to pay, mix up your points of entry and exit, so you don't cross the same border every time. Among other things, this is a great opportunity to explore neighbouring countries by land, air and sea!

The Schengen Area

Note that some countries have rules that are less amenable to digital nomads. Non-Europeans travelling to most EU countries enter under the Schengen Agreement, which allows up to 90 days of visa-free travel within the Schengen Area in one 180-day period.

This covers 26 countries, so leaving Estonia for Finland, for example, will still count as part of the same 90-day entry into the Schengen Area, and you'll still need to be out of the Schengen Area for several months after using up your 90-day allowance before you can come back in for a further 90 days. The EU states of Bulgaria, Croatia, Cyprus and Romania are not part of the Schengen Area, so entering one of these states is one way to prolong a European stay.

TOP TIP

'If you plan to stay somewhere for longer than the standard tourist visa allows, check out the regulations ahead of time. Some countries allow extensions of tourist visas, but there are often conditions. Overstaying is best avoided – there might only be a small fine on departure, but overstaying can make it harder to re-enter the country in future.'

Joe Bindloss, travel writer

© XTEIANA LAZUNOVA / ISTOCK / GETTY IMAGES

TRAVEL INSURANCE

In a perfect world, every trip would be as smooth as sipping whiskey. In the real world, mishaps occur all the time, so nomads need to be prepared. You might fall ill. You might lose your wallet. Worse still, somebody could walk off with the laptop containing all your work files. Travel insurance is pretty much essential if you hope to have any piece of mind while working overseas.

Always make sure that your policy covers medical treatment and evacuation in the event of a medical emergency or a natural disaster. Keep the hotline number handy – your insurer may be able to advise on reputable local medical facilities as well as handling claims.

Comprehensive medical cover

Some destinations may have reciprocal health agreements with your home country (be sure to carry any paperwork confirming eligibility) but most healthcare systems around the world are pay-as-you-go. Take out travel insurance to cover any medical costs in an emergency, and check if the insurance company pays providers directly, or if you need to pay up front first and claim back later.

Sorry, you're not covered

Travel insurance will cover you for most problems overseas, but it's important to be aware of exclusions. Most policies will not cover replacement flights if the airline you are booked on goes bust, and many insurers exclude countries where your home government has issued an 'avoid all travel' warning. Always check the latest travel warnings from the British Foreign & Commonwealth Office (www.gov.uk/foreign-travel-advice), the US State Department (http://travel.state.gov) or the equivalent government department in your own country.

What about my gear?

As a digital nomad, you're likely to be toting some expensive tech. Make sure your policy covers the full replacement cost of valuable items, such as laptops, cameras and mobile phones. High-value items may need to be specifically listed in the policy.

How about my down-time?

Life isn't all work, work, work. Make sure that your travel insurance covers you for any activities you plan to do on your trip; there may be special exclusions for adventure sports and other risky activities. When renting a vehicle, stick to companies that provide insurance cover for damage to the vehicle, and medical costs and damage if you collide with anybody else.

Nomad-friendly travel insurance

Some travel insurance policies are only valid if you are a legal resident of the country where the issuing company is based, and others only cover trips of up to a maximum of 30, 60 or 90 days. Look for nomad-friendly policies from companies such as Safety Wing (www.safetywing.com), World Nomads (www.worldnomads.com) and True Traveller (www.truetraveller.com). Always check the small print; some policies place a limit on how many times you can return home during the period of cover.

FIFTEEN ITEMS EVERY DIGITAL NOMAD SHOULD CARRY

Some pieces of technology you can find almost everywhere. Other things can't be had for love nor money. Here's a list of essential tech that should be part of every digital nomad toolkit.

© 2020, OUTPOST CANGGU, BALI

A universal travel adapter plug (or several of them) – locally made adaptors often wobble in sockets like a loose tooth.

Surge-protection – the last thing you want is a power surge that fries all your tech in one sizzle.

A multiplug or power strip – if your room only has one plug socket, you're still covered.

An external hard drive, USB stick or memory card for critical back ups.

A 1m ethernet cable – co-working spaces should have them, but there's no harm having your own.

Spare USB leads – carry spares of leads with the right connectors in case of broken wires.

A spare laptop power supply – finding a charger for a specific laptop can be surprisingly difficult.

Noise-cancelling headphones – instant meeting-room quiet, whenever you need it.

A battery power pack – essential kit for keeping your phone or tablet alive when you can't find a socket.

An unlocked, back-up phone – even a calls-only phone can keep your business moving.

Earphones with a microphone – for Skype and WhatsApp calls on the go.

An external mouse – if your trackpad goes down, your business doesn't have to.

A folding keyboard – you won't want to use it every day, but it's a useful fallback.

A portable laptop stand – you won't have HR emailing to remind you about your posture.

Universal card reader – for getting photos off camera cards, and data from memory cards.

© 2020, OUTPOST CANGGU, BALI

Tech tips for digital nomads

The digital nomad life is only possible because of three inventions: the laptop, the mobile phone and the internet. With this life-changing tech, you can take your entire business on the trail and work from almost anywhere with an internet connection. So it makes sense to give some thought to the technology you are taking on the road.

Mac or Windows?

Every laptop user has to make some binary decisions – are you a Beatles or Stones fan, a dog person or a cat person, Apple or Microsoft? Apple has a long history of pioneering tech and design, creating sleek, silver machines that have become the standard tools in industries such as publishing, photography and videography. Devotees swear that Apple products look better and work better, but they also cost more than the alternatives, and it can be tricky finding parts and support in some countries as a travelling digital nomad.

Microsoft-based laptops are cheaper, often lighter, and easy to find parts for almost anywhere in the world, and they're the default tool for gaming and coding, though many devs opt out of the Windows environment and run alternative operating systems, such as Linux. Which system you use will depend on what you use your laptop and mobile phone for, your budget, and ultimately what works for you as an individual.

With the cost factor, many nomads go with Microsoft machines simply because they're less expensive, easier to fix or replace, and less of a magnet for thieves – always a consideration when your entire working life is on the laptop in front of you.

Smartphone smarts

For mobile, the contest is between Apple's iOS and Google's Android, but both offer a vast array of apps and good synchronisation between mobiles and laptops. A more

© 2020, THE HIVE, SINGAPORE

important consideration is whether the phone will work with local SIM cards to cut down on expensive roaming data costs. The ideal digital nomad phone is not locked to any particular network, and has dual SIM slots, meaning you can keep your home number active and plug in local SIMs as you go.

Protecting your tech

As a digital nomad, the worst thing that can happen (shark attacks and exploding volcanoes aside) is losing your laptop. Even if your work is backed up to the cloud, losing the most important tool of your trade can be a major obstacle to running your business. Always take out sufficient travel insurance to cover the cost of replacing or repairing all of your essential tech and back up your phone

contacts to the cloud, including the hotline number for your insurance company, serial numbers for essential software, and details of high-value items you are travelling with.

Insurance companies may be able to replace the physical machines that were stolen, lost or crushed by an elephant, but they can't replace your data, so always keep back ups. Sync your phone to your laptop or the cloud regularly, make daily back-ups from your laptop, and keep external storage devices separate from the machine you are working on. When you fly on

to the next nomad destination, keep your tech in your carry-on luggage, rather than gambling on it arriving safely via the hold.

Backing it up

As well as workplace tech, you'll need a system for backing up your valuable files in case anything happens to your precious phone or laptop. The default for many users is the cloud, where everything is saved to secure servers in vast data centres dotted around the world. Many mobile phones back up to the cloud by default, and thousands of nomads rely on

ONLINE SAFETY TIPS

★ Use a PIN or password to lock phone, laptop and other devices when not used for a few minutes.

★ Smart passwords mix upper- and lower-case letters and numbers.

★ Update passwords regularly, and don't use the same password for multiple sites.

★ Upgrade to biometric ID checks (eg fingerprint login) wherever available.

★ Turn off auto-connect to avoid unsafe wi-fi.

★ Turn off Bluetooth and wi-fi when not in use.

★ Enable two-factor authentication and verification to protect sensitive accounts.

★ Confirm which is the correct network before you log on – scammers often set up networks with similar sounding names to lure in victims.

★ Disable automatic file sharing, unless you actually need to share them with someone.

★ Download and activate tracking apps for your devices.

© 2020, PUNSPACE, CHIANG MAI / PH. JEKITA

free-to-use cloud-based storage, such as Google Drive (www.google.com/drive) and DropBox (www.dropbox.com).

The disadvantage of cloud-based storage is that you need a net connection to access your data, which can be a headache in countries where the power supply is unreliable, and you may have to pay for extra storage if you burn through a lot of data. Using external storage devices – portable hard drives, USB drives or memory cards – is one alternative, though you have to keep these physical items safe from theft and damage. In practice, most nomads do a bit of both.

The software jungle

Some industries depend on expensive pieces of software like InDesign, Photoshop and Premiere Pro, but for nomads on a budget, there are cheaper or free alternatives. Much of Photoshop's impressive functionality can be found in the free, open-source application Gimp (www.gimp.org), and the once-unassailable position held by Microsoft's Office has been undermined by free-to-use online apps, such as Google Docs (https://docs.google.com). With a bit of searching online, it's possible to furnish your laptop with a full suite of office applications without ever going near an expensive software licence.

TECH SAFE TRAVEL

In today's interconnected world, thieves don't need to physically grab your laptop to steal your address book, money and identity. Public wi-fi connections are particularly prone to abuse, thanks to the insecure nature of WPA2 encryption, so cyber security should be at the heart of your business. Running a digital business remotely means sharing and accessing sensitive financial information that thieves would love to get their hands on if you give them the chance.

Be virtually secure

The default protection for most digital nomads is a Virtual Private Network (VPN), which adds extra layers of security and encryption to data sent over public networks. Software providers such as Express VPN (www.expressvpn.com) and Nord VPN (www.nordvpn.com) offer paid-for networks that will help keep your data secure, and also let you circumvent location-specific blocks on websites, so you can access the full breadth of the web, or log on to your BBC iPlayer or Amazon Prime, wherever you are.

Don't catch a bug

Anti-virus software is another must-have for the jobbing digital nomad, so make sure you have up-to-date protection – and don't make the mistake of assuming that 'Macs don't get viruses', as many users have found to their cost. Update your software whenever a new version is available; many updates are just the latest step in the ongoing arms race between software producers and hackers.

Setting out your stall

Okay, so you've set yourself up as a digital nomad, in the perfect nomad city, with the perfect co-working space. Now you can just sit back and watch the work roll in, right? Guess again...

As a roaming remote worker, you don't have a shop window to lure in passing customers, so you'll need to set out your stall online. The internet is where you find new clients and where new clients find you, and you'll need a highly visible online presence to sell your skills and expertise to people who are thinking of paying for your services. The internet is jammed with online businesses competing for passing internet traffic, so making your business stand out from the pack is critical to carve out a niche in this crowded marketplace. Here are some things to consider to get on the radar of potential clients.

TOP TIP

'When I first started out writing, I had to chase every project, but as I built up a body of work, with a particular focus on India and South Asia, my website became more and more useful. Before long, people who had read my guidebooks and articles were emailing me through my website with commissions, without me having to do any chasing at all.'

Joe Bindloss, travel writer, www.bindloss.co.uk

Build a blog

A blog is a different kind of creature – a place to host fresh new content, create a unique brand and build up an army (hopefully) of followers who come back regularly to check out your latest posts. It's this traffic that helps you sell advertising space and make money from your posts. For some bloggers, a blog can be enough to fund an entire digital nomad lifestyle. However, it's important not to duplicate content between your blog and website, as both sites will be penalised by search engines.

© MASKOT / GETTY IMAGES

Build a website

Websites and blogs can serve different purposes and provide different revenue streams, so it helps to have both. One of the most practical uses for a traditional 'this is my company' website is as your online resume – a place to advertise your achievements and send to clients who want to check out your portfolio. You'll need an eye-catching landing page, a portfolio page with past projects, an easy-to-navigate hierarchy that doesn't waste visitor's time, and a contact page that lets people message you directly, with links to your LinkedIn and social media profiles.

Build your brand

Even as a lone traveller with a laptop, you're a brand, and you want people to remember your name and associate it with excellence in whatever trade you're involved in. Some people choose a snappy nomad name, riffing on themes that people connect with the lifestyle. Others trade under their real names or a business-like company moniker, often with missing letters – or should that be 'lettrs' – for brand association with the digital revolution.

The golden rule is to find your niche. If you're selling your coding skills, make your brand, website and blog all about coding, rather than trying to cover coding, dog-walking and interior design under one umbrella. If you work in multiple fields, create multiple brands and multiple websites, each speaking to a specific market.

Advertise

Having built a brand, you need people to know about it. Get the word out there, on LinkedIn (www.linkedin.com), on social media, on industry forums and even via traditional paid-for advertising. A blog can be a great tool for building your reputation as an expert voice; and sharing your posts on Twitter, Facebook and other platforms, and contributing to threads on your specialist topics can add to the buzz.

Network

Every business needs a network, and digital nomads are in a unique position to get in touch with other freelancers, start-up owners and digital entrepreneurs to build their profile, share ideas and create new opportunities. Many new connections happen face-to-face in co-working spaces, but they also happen on specialist online forums and Facebook groups for digital nomads. Remember the age-old principle of mutual back-scratching – people are more likely to share your content and posts if you share theirs, so talk to your network about ways you can help each other grow. It's what makes the business world go round.

LET YOUR FINGERS DO THE SEARCHING

Often, finding freelance work is a case of searching for gigs online and putting yourself forward, so take full advantage of the web to track down freelance opportunities. Visit job sites for freelancers and remote workers and use varied search terms to find jobs within your specialist area – so, search for 'office support' as well as 'virtual assistant'. Don't overlook LinkedIn (www.linkedin.com); mention freelancing prominently in your profile, approach potential clients and connect with new people in your industry who may need your skills.

You don't have to wait for someone to post a 'freelancer wanted' ad. If there's a company you want to work for, make the first move and offer your services. Just make sure you target your pitches to the right person, in a way that catches their attention, emphasising all the amazing things you can do to help their business (backed up with examples of past work). Here are some of the biggest job sites for freelance and remote work:

★ **CareerBuilder** www.careerbuilder.com
★ **Freelancer** www.freelancer.com
★ **Indeed** www.indeed.com
★ **Flexjobs** www.flexjobs.com
★ **Fiverr** www.fiverr.com
★ **Monster** www.monster.com
★ **People Per Hour** www.peopleperhour.com
★ **Reed** www.reedglobal.com
★ **Remote** www.remote.com
★ **Upwork** www.upwork.com
★ **We Work Remotely** www.weworkremotely.com

ON THE ROAD

© JOHANNES HULSCH / 500P

Arriving in your destination

There's no feeling quite like stepping off the aeroplane for the first time in a new destination. The feel of the air. The colour of the light. The sound of a strange language. The way people dress. The smell of aviation fuel as you leave the aircraft. With excitement coursing through your veins, you're prepped and primed to dive in and make your digital life a success.

It would be tempting to give yourself a couple of days of downtime to ease into things slowly and get used to the destination, but it's easy for those few days to turn into a few weeks, and for your digital nomad journey to turn into a fun-filled holiday rather than a serious attempt to earn a living while travelling.

It's usually more productive to start as you mean to go on, getting straight down to the business of setting up your remote-working life as soon as you set foot on the tarmac. You'll be here for a while, so there'll be plenty of time to smell the roses and see the sights.

ENSURING A SMOOTH LANDING

To get off on the right foot, plan your arrival to minimise stress and hassle. Do plenty of research ahead of time – online, via guidebooks, and by talking to other nomads via Facebook groups and forums – and work out a seamless route from the airport to your first overnight stop.

★ **Fly overnight, land in the morning** The best flights run overnight, giving you time to sleep, and land in the morning, giving you hours of daylight to adjust.

★ **Don't arrive after dark** Things will be closed, taxi fares are higher, and you're more at risk of crime and simply getting lost in an unfamiliar city.

★ **Pre-book the first night's accommodation** You don't want to be wandering around lost in a strange city trying to find somewhere to stay after a long-haul flight.

★ **Arrange an airport pick-up** Many hotels, hostels and co-living spaces can send a driver to meet you at the airport, taking away the stress of navigating public transport or haggling with mercenary cab drivers.

★ **Make a tech plan** Research internet access and mobile phone coverage ahead of time, so you can land, grab a local SIM and get straight online.

★ **Think about the money** Airport foreign exchange desks often give poor rates; change enough cash to get you through day one (or use an ATM) and worry about the big transactions later.

A PERFECT FIRST DAY

It's your first day in your dream destination so make it count. Set your alarm for early and use the first 24 hours to get firmly acquainted with the city that will be your new home.

Take a walk at first light

Don't sleep your life away! The first few hours after dawn are the best time to explore before the commuter crush kicks in. Pick up a local map, or download one onto your phone, and set out on foot to get the measure of your local neighbourhood.

Find somewhere great for breakfast

Cafe breakfasts are likely to be a big part of your routine as a digital nomad, so check out the quality of the local cafe scene, with a particular eye on the speed of the wi-fi connection. Do some research ahead of time for top recommendations from local bloggers and fellow nomads.

Get acquainted with public transport

Unless you founded Facebook and can afford to get around by limo, public transport is going to feature big in your remote working life. Devote some time to getting around by train, tram or bus to work out how networks connect and how to pay for your ride.

Hunt down a street food lunch

Eating in the street is one of the great pleasures of travel, and nothing makes you feel like an insider quite like finding the best place in town for a bowl of pho noodles or a hot empanada. Check local food markets and food streets, and consult food blogs for insider tips.

Relax in a local park

Every city slicker needs some greenery now and again, so check out the local parks and find your new favourite place to head for picnics, calming walks or a morning jog before heading to the (shared) office.

Investigate local co-working spaces

You came here to work, so set aside some time to buzz around local co-working spaces to check out the facilities. Test the internet connections, investigate the social calendar, and introduce yourself to some of your prospective co-workers; this could be the start of a beautiful working relationship.

Find an authentic local meal

Every city is famous for something, so celebrate your first day in town by trying the local speciality. How posh you go is up to you but, often, the best food in town is served not at the swanky place with the besuited maître d' but at the family trattoria on the corner.

Find your new local

It will probably take time before the local bar staff know your drinks order, but a mini bar crawl in search of your new local watering hole is a great way to end a day of exploring. Skip the traveller hangouts for locals' haunts and go native in the best possible way.

Accommodation

Accommodation will be the biggest single cost of nomadic life, so plan ahead. Being a temporary resident isn't like passing through on holiday; hotels and hostels drain budgets, and you'll need your own living space to feel fully at home. Location is key: if you have to travel halfway across a city to reach cafes and co-working spaces, transport costs may outweigh savings on rent. Here are some options to mull over.

 ## HOTELS & HOSTELS

Rooms in hotels and hostels are easy to find, and plenty of nomads start off a trip with a couple of nights in standard tourist accommodation. On the plus side, you'll normally have access to free wi-fi and breakfasts, and free tea and (instant) coffee. On the down side, you'll have a small living area, no kitchen, and you'll be sleeping and working in the same space, which can have a negative effect on sleep patterns.

Hotels can also feel isolating (ask any travelling sales person) and hostels offer company but limited privacy and security. Long-term, the costs of either can add up, though you may be able to negotiate a discount for a long stay. For listings of hostels worldwide, try HostelWorld.com (www.hostelworld.com). Good booking sites for last minute, discounted hotel rooms include Hotel Tonight (www.hoteltonight.com) and Booking.com (www.booking.com).

 ## AIRBNB

The world's most popular room booking site, Airbnb has rooms and apartments rented directly by owners in 191 countries. Many veteran digital nomads begin every new stop in an Airbnb before finding somewhere more permanent. Many rooms and apartments come with wi-fi, and are run by friendly hosts who can help you plug quickly into the local area. For a few days or weeks, Airbnb can be very cost-effective, but it can be uneconomical for longer stays.

 ## RENTED ROOMS & APARTMENTS

So long as you have internet access, a rented apartment or a room in a house-share is a win-win for digital nomads. You'll have your own space to work, rest and play, and kitchen access will cut down eating costs. With house-shares, you'll also have instant company – though this can be a blessing or a curse.

Per-night costs for both are often significantly lower than other forms of accommodation, but do factor in the cost of heating, electricity and other bills. If there's a phone line and internet access, this will be another extra, and if there isn't, you may have to arrange a connection through a local provider.

Find apartments online: through real estate agents, or holiday rental sites like HolidayLettings (www.holidaylettings.com) and HomeAway (www.homeaway.com). Another good option is chatting to fellow nomads and expats at co-working spaces or via Facebook groups. GoBeHere (www.gobehere.com) and Nomad Rental (www.nomadrental.com) are specialist platforms for accommodation deliberately angled toward digital nomads.

CO-LIVING

Co-living falls somewhere between co-working and living in a shared house – think of it as a commune for remote workers, modelled on Mark Zuckerberg's start-up house in Palo Alto. Many co-working spaces offer co-living, either on site or close by. You typically get a room with a bathroom, and access to shared spaces to eat, work and relax, plus faster than average internet connection. You get a great sense of shared purpose, as everyone is working in the same way, and a social buzz that can break down the isolation of remote working. But it isn't always the cheapest option (though residents might have discounted access to other work spaces and meeting rooms), and you'll have much less privacy than in a rented apartment. Visit CoLiving (www.coliving.com), Digital Nomad House (www.digitalnomadhouse.net) or Outside (www.outsite.co) to start searching options.

TOP TIP

'I've spent long periods house sitting, and not having to pay housing costs takes the pressure off. The most surprising house sit was on the Isle of Mull, Scotland. Despite it being winter and quite remote, I fell in love with the place, and I've been back several times, though the lack of mobile service and super-slow internet is challenging.'

Doug Murray, content creator & marketing professional at www. dougmurrayproductions. com

COUCH-SURFING

Couch-surfing is a favourite option for budget travellers, but it isn't perfect for the nomad life, as it means limited personal space, an unpredictable working environment, and being dependent on the goodwill and internet connection of a host you've never met. On the other hand, you get to meet some interesting people. Find sofas seeking sleepers at Couchsurfing.com (www.couchsurfing.com).

HOUSE-SITTING

House-sitting is enticing. It's usually free, and you'll have a whole home or apartment – some are palatial compared to standard digital nomad digs. On the flip side, you'll have to keep the place how owners like it rather than creating a space that works for you. Find options via Housecarers (www.housecarers.com), House Sitting World (www.housesittingworld.com) and MindMyHouse (www.mindmyhouse.com).

Eating & drinking

Food is one of the great pleasures of travel, and finding local haunts and street food favourites is part of the fun. But eating out for every meal will ratchet up costs, so make sure your living arrangements include kitchen access. Eating alone can take a little getting used to; many solo diners bring a book, a tablet or even a laptop.

© JUSTIN FOULKES / LONELY PLANET

Eat local

Eating alone in a fine-dining restaurant can be a weird experience, but solo diners rarely feel out of place in fast-paced, busy local restaurants full of noise, chatter and bustle. You can immerse yourself in local cuisine, not the toned-down-for-tourists version, and save money to boot.

To find the best places, ask staff at hostels and co-working spaces, talk to fellow residents in house-shares (or people in the street), and use nomad networking and social sessions to pick up tips. And follow your nose and ears to local venues with queues stretching out of the doors, amazing smells coming out of the kitchens, and a babble of conversation.

Acquire a local palate

If you insist on eating food from your native home, your shopping and dining bills will spiral. There's always a premium on imported goods, and things like cheese, bacon and wine can be expensive luxuries. Stick to what locals eat, however, and your grocery bills can be so low as to be almost negligible, particularly if you shop at local markets rather than expat supermarkets. Wander around and get a sense of what is cheap and expensive for people on a local budget; fish is often cheaper than meat or poultry, while fruit and vegetables can be so cheap that it's difficult to buy less than a carrier-bag full.

Do a cooking course

Those piles of green leaves and tangled roots in local markets can be intimidating and mysterious. What the heck are those things? Salad ingredients, herbs, vegetables, medicine? To demystify local produce, sign up for a cooking course with a guided market visit. In just a couple of days, you can learn a whole new repertoire of inexpensive go-to meals, prepared using exotic local ingredients, that will blow the roof off your familiar diet of spaghetti Bolognaise and mac 'n' cheese.

When in Rome

Some countries follow a predictable breakfast, lunch and dinner routine at similar times to back home. Other countries rush through breakfast as soon as it gets light, leaving supper till long after dark. If you adjust your internal chronometer to match the local dining clock, you won't get caught out if, for example, all the cafes in town close on Friday morning as everyone goes to the mosque. Be ready for Ramadan (Ramazan) in Islamic countries; during the holy month of fasting, eating and drinking anything apart from water during the day may be prohibited, and restaurants will only open when the fast is broken at sunset.

Street food feasts

Travellers are often put off street food by a justifiable fear of stomach bugs, but it can be the most delicious food of all, sold at a fraction of sit-down restaurant prices. Ask locals about the area's best street treats, and follow some simple rules to avoid stomach upsets: stick to food you can see being freshly prepared in front of you, avoid ice and salads unless you're sure the water is safe, clean hands with wipes or sanitizer before you eat, and only visit stalls that are busy with locals. Seek out dedicated street food markets and hawker courts; food stalls around train and bus stations and produce markets; and lunchtime snack stops in business districts.

© I.S.S PHOTOGRAPHY / GETTY IMAGES

Allergies, intolerances & special diets

Other countries may not have the same awareness of allergies and intolerances as you are used to at home. If you have a serious allergy or intolerance, carry the necessary emergency treatments and cards explaining your condition in the local language – visit www.selectwisely.com or www.allergytranslation.com for more advice.

© LINDSAY LAUCKNER GUNDLOCK / LONELY PLANET

Vegans & vegetarians

Being vegan or vegetarian can bring its own challenges. The phrase 'vegetarian' is often shorthand for 'with vegetables' rather than 'without meat' and the use of meat-, chicken- or fish stock can be ubiquitous. Even where vegetarianism is common, the notion of a milk- and egg-free diet may be a novelty. Sticking to religious restaurants can be a solution – Buddhist restaurants in Asia are often vegetarian, and Jain and South Indian restaurants proudly advertise their 'veg' or 'pure-veg' status.

Choosing your workspace

Having decided which city to use as a base, the next big decision is where you'll work. That idyllic image of working at your laptop on the beach is a bit of a fantasy – you won't be able to see the screen clearly, and where is the wi-fi coming from? Real-life nomads choose a workspace with free wi-fi and a quiet environment. Here are some tips.

The coffee shop boardroom

Coffee shops have a lot of advantages. The wi-fi is normally fast and free and, outside of busy lunchtimes and the morning/evening commutes, they offer a calm working environment. Being in a public space with other people can also break down the isolation of working alone in a flat or rented room. On the flip side, you'll have to pay for drinks or snacks to use the wi-fi, and not every coffee shop will be happy with you nursing a single cappuccino while you use the wi-fi for a whole working day.

Coffee shop meetings are common these days, but there's little privacy, so this is not a great environment for talking about money or having sensitive phone or video conferencing conversations. Also be aware that cafe wi-fi networks are public, so be cautious about sending personal information unless you are using a VPN (Virtual Private Network). Power supplies can also be a problem; unless there's a socket in the wall next to your table, your work time may be limited by your battery life.

The (rented) home office

There's nothing to stop you using your hostel, hotel or apartment as a workspace, and it can bring down your costs significantly. However, you may feel like a bit of a hermit if you spend all your time in one space, and there are numerous studies showing that living and working in the same small space can affect sleep patterns and stress. You will of course need access to the internet, provided for free in many hostels and hotels but not always available in rented rooms or apartments unless you pay extra.

If you have a local SIM on a 4G network, this can be a low-cost solution, but for a reliably fast internet connection, you may need to sign up with a local Internet Service Provider (ISP) and many packages are for a minimum of a year. On the other hand, you'll have plenty of privacy for calls and facetime meetings, and you can always mix it up by working in cafes and co-working spaces.

Co-working a go-go

Co-working has been dramatically reinvented from the days when dubious lettings agents worked from Regus shared offices on industrial estates. Today's co-working spaces are bright, creative environments with meeting rooms, booths for phone and Skype calls and chill-out spaces (typically with beanbag chairs – it's part of the culture). You also get a cafe or a kitchen, and most co-working spaces offer internet speeds that are in orders of magnitude faster than public wi-fi, so this is the default way of working for nomads in data-hungry fields, such as programming, graphic design and video production.

WHAT TO LOOK FOR FROM A CO-WORKING SPACE

When you look around for a co-working space, seek out the following desirable features:

★ An internet connection with download speeds of 100 Mbps or greater.
★ A choice of hot desks or private offices.
★ Meeting rooms and phone booths for privacy.
★ 24/7 access for members.
★ Greenery and natural light.
★ Low noise levels to encourage productivity.
★ A cafe for screen breaks.
★ A kitchen, for cheap homemade lunches.
★ Regular networking events and social meetups.
★ Good security, to reduce the chance of someone walking off with your valuable tech.
★ Back-up generators in countries with unreliable power supplies.
★ A good atmosphere.

Almost all co-working spaces offer day passes and cheaper weekly, monthly or annual memberships. There's normally a choice of hot desks (with an ergonomic chair, ethernet cable and power supply) or private offices; the latter are in-demand and expensive: finding a hot desk for less than US$150 per month anywhere in the world can be a challenge. The biggest perk is the social scene. Co-working spaces are great places to network, and most run regular workshops, networking sessions and social meetups.

Finding a co-working space

Search specialist co-working sites such as CoWorker (www.coworker.com) or the app Croissant (www.getcroissant.com). Joining Facebook groups for expats and digital nomads in your chosen city is another good way to seek out recommendations, or Google the city name and 'co-working' for listings and blog posts on local co-working spaces.

Other public spaces

Many civic buildings provide free or low-price internet access: public libraries almost always provide desks for working and a famously quiet work environment. Bus and train stations, airports, museums and fast food restaurants are also good (if noisy) places to find free wi-fi. Traditional internet cafes are going the way of the dodo, but they can be a useful back-up.

© 2020, OUTPOST CANGGU, BALI

TIPS FOR FINDING WI-FI

As a digital nomad, you need an internet connection like a barracuda needs water. If the wi-fi is free, even better. You could always wander the streets looking for cafes with a wi-fi sticker on the window, but as this is your livelihood, it's better to scope out hotspots in advance. Here are some top tips for finding public internet.

Use an app

Free app WiFi Finder (iOS or Android) offers map-based searches for free wi-fi worldwide. You can download maps for use offline (handy for cities without 4G) and the database is kept up to date. WiFi Map (www.wifimap. io) and Wiman (www.wiman.me) are also popular.

Be a bookworm

Public libraries are almost guaranteed to have free or inexpensive internet access, as well as quiet spaces to work. You'll find free wi-fi in many other public buildings, and also in malls, museums, and transport hubs.

Flexiroam

Another option for eager roamers is Flexiroam (www.flexiroam.com), an app with a miniature SIM that physically sticks over your existing SIM card, offering cut-price roaming internet in 140 countries, with a validity of one year.

Use the web

App versions of web-based hotspot databases include OpenWiFiSpots (www. openwifispots.com; worldwide maps via user reports); Boingo (www.boingo.com; subscription-based, with a million hotspots worldwide); WiFi Free Spot (www. wififreespot.com; global listings).

Tether your phone

It's not free, but if all else fails, you can use your phone as a modem by tethering it via Bluetooth or a USB cable to your laptop; you'll need a 3G or 4G connection.

Follow the chains

All Apple stores, and most branches of Starbucks and McDonalds, offer free wi-fi; connections are normally reliable.

Carry your own hotspot

Another option for when you absolutely must have a connection is a portable wi-fi hotspot. These glorified mobile phones use a SIM card to get you online and many need a data subscription. An unlocked hotspot will work with local SIM cards, cutting down your internet costs.

TOP TIP

'If possible, buy a local SIM card with internet access - this means you have a backup internet connection if the connection in your accommodation or cafe fails. Its usually cheaper to buy a local pay-as-you-go, so check out SIM card dataplans in advance.'

Piotr Gryko, remote software developer, www.piotrgryko.com

CONNECTING WITH OTHER DIGITAL NOMADS

Being a digital nomad doesn't have to mean being a recluse, even if you're working for yourself rather than being part of a team. Plugging into the local nomad network is a great way to find out what other people are doing and get tips for great places to eat, sleep and work, as well as finding a new social circle.

Co-working

Co-working spaces offer dedicated networking sessions, workshops and social events, and their cafes, kitchens and chill-out zones are great places to to connect with other destination-independent workers.

Facebook groups

Most cities popular with digital nomads have dedicated Facebook groups where you can plug into a huge pool of local wisdom; expat groups are handy for more general advice and local connections. Search for the name of your city and 'digital nomads' or 'expats'.

Co-Living

Co-living is co-working taken to the next level. You'll dive straight into a like-minded community, but being part of a preformed group can be limiting when it comes to engaging with local people and your destination – so do extend beyond your immediate circle.

Nomad List

As well as its plethora of resources – co-working searches, city/cost of living reviews – Nomad List (www.nomadlist. com) has a popular members' forum and a buzzing chat group and Slack channel. Membership costs US$9.99 per month, less for long-term packages.

Meetups

Most co-working spaces run regular meetups for remote workers, some with a business focus and some with a social bent – drinks nights, pizza evenings, activities, group hikes and the like. Any space can tell you what they have in the calendar. Lots of professional and social events for roaming workers are arranged via the website Meetup (www.meetup.com) or ask around about events on forums for digital nomads.

TOP TIP

'Don't get lonely. Every time you move to a new place, make an active effort to make friends. Couch-surfing meetups generally operate in almost every city in the world and are a great way to meet locals. Searching for Facebook events in a new location can also be a great way to see what's going on in a new city.' *Piotr Gryko, remote software developer, www.piotrgryko.com*

Group nomading

Companies such as WiFi Tribe (www.wifitribe.co) offer organised co-living packages, with a global network of shared or private rooms that you can drop into for a month at a time and be instantly part of a working and social community. However, prices are high and the gap-year vibe can be a bit limiting for those seeking an independent life. Remote Year (www. remoteyear.com) and Hacker Paradise (www.hackerparadise. org) run similar programmes.

Getting around

Living somewhere is not the same as just passing through. Those impulsive late-night taxi rides can soon add up, and many nomads find themselves living like locals do and relying on public transport. Don't overlook walking or renting a bike; nothing gives you quite such a strong sense of the layout of a new place as pootling around under your own steam.

Google Maps

Google Maps (https://maps.google.com) is an invaluable tool for finding your way anywhere in the world. You can plot routes between places, measure distances, drop pins and download offline maps to your phone.

Use taxi-hailing apps

Are there any? Are they reliable? Uber (www.uber.com) is taking the world by storm, but many countries have their own local apps with more drivers and shorter waiting times. In North America, try Lyft (www.lyft.com) and Curb (https://mobileapp.gocurb.com); in India, take a punt on Ola (www.olacabs.com). Didi Chuxing (www.didiglobal.com) rules the roost in China, while Line (www.linecorp.com) does the same job in Japan, and GrabTaxi (www.grab.com) has a wide reach in Singapore, Malaysia, Indonesia and other parts of Southeast Asia.

Get a local pass

In 2013, Tallinn became the first city in the world to offer free public transport for residents. Most cities don't go that far, but almost all offer some kind of pass or smartcard offering discounted public transport fares. Some require proof of residency; for others you just buy a smartcard and load it up with credit. Some modes of transport burn through money faster than others, with underground and overground train networks topping the costs table.

Rent a scooter or motorcycle

In Asia, and much of the rest of the world, motorcycles, mopeds and scooters are king. These versatile vehicles are cheap to rent, easy to park and perfect for navigating narrow and crowded streets. Stick to rental companies that provide insurance for damage to the vehicle, and cover for medical costs and damage if you collide with someone else. Those no questions asked, leave-your-passport-as-deposit rental shops are best avoided.

Work local

Commuting can eat into your profits. Live close to your workspace and the savings made by walking instead of taking the train soon add up. Some co-working spaces offer co-living in the same location, though there's something to be said for keeping your work and home separate in terms of being able to turn off at the end of a workday.

Work-life balance

On a holiday, there's no reason not to splash some cash on the top experiences and worry about the cost later, but as a remote-working resident, you have a business to run and a budget to keep to. It pays to be a bit more disciplined and save the splurges for special occasions – not every day needs to be a treat day.

Treat yourself

Build exercise and rewards into your weekly schedule, but do take a day off for something special occasionally. The Toggl (www.toggl.com) app can help balance work and leisure time.

Take a walk in the park

Most public parks are calm spaces where you can take a walk, breathe deep, exhale – and forget about the chaos of the city for a moment. Entry fees, if they exist at all, are nominal, and city parks are great places to see locals at play and gain a deeper understanding of what makes the place tick.

Go wild

Outdoorsy types who work close to their favourite surf breaks, trekking trails or climbing crags have free adventure on tap. If you're crazy about climbing, bonkers about BASE jumping or fanatical about fishing, choosing a hub where you can enjoy your favourite activity for free will make your down-time as rewarding as your work time.

Hit the beach

If you've chosen a seaside digital hub, you've hit the relaxation jackpot. Your co-working space could be minutes from swimming, snorkelling, surfing or just sunbathing on the sand. You don't have to be near the sea, either: many cities have river beaches or artificial beaches in parks.

Explore new neighbourhoods

One perk of being a stranger in a strange land is the chance to go somewhere new every day and feel like a proper explorer. Use weekends and days off to mount expeditions to new neighbourhoods, to seek out amazing street art, spectacular street food, no-holds-barred nightlife and perhaps even somewhere new to live if you tire of your existing crib.

Get some culture

Museums are on a mission to educate, and many of the world's top cultural institutions are free to visit, opening up a world of art, culture and history. Even where museums charge a fee, as a resident remote worker, you'll have the flexibility to visit on the one free day per week, or come after hours when entry is half-price.

TOP TIP

'As a freelancer, it can be difficult to know when to work and when to switch off. It took me a long time to let go of the 9–5 mentality after I realised I was most productive at night, but once I gave myself permission to work unconventional office hours, I could explore during the day without guilt. Don't be afraid to find your own rhythm.'

Emily McAuliffe,
travel writer & copywriter,
www.emilymcauliffe.com

BEING A STRANGER IN A STRANGE LAND

On day one, being somewhere new can make you feel like a celebrity, or a jungle explorer, uncovering a lost city for the first time. By day number 180, some of the shine will probably have worn off. There's a reason nomads of a feather flock together: having the adventurous spirit to go somewhere new doesn't change the fact that it's comforting to spend time with people who share the same life experiences as you do.

To get the best out of being a digital nomad, find time in your life for a bit of both. Don't be afraid to branch out on your own and dive into the local way of life, but don't feel bad about retreating sometimes to the comforting company of fellow nomads and expats, to share the surprises, frustrations and discoveries that wouldn't be the same for someone already living there full time.

TIPS FOR ADJUSTING TO A STRANGE LAND

Being a digital nomad doesn't have to mean being a recluse, even if you're working for yourself rather than being part of a team. Plugging into the local nomad network is a great way to find out what other people are doing and get tips for great places to eat, sleep and work, as well as finding a new social circle.

★ Culture from the old country

With the growth of digital entertainment, the traveller tradition of heading to the British Council or the Alliance Francaise for a film from home or an evening cultural show has rather fallen from favour, but it's likely to be a much more social occasion than sitting in your apartment with a pirate DVD of *Game of Thrones*. Check the noticeboards at cultural centres run by foreign governments for listings of upcoming events or attend special screenings and shows at local universities, and you'll feel less of a stranger and more part of a scene.

★ The familiar taste of home

Nothing eases homesickness quite like the familiar flavours of home. Across the world, expats make micro-pilgrimages to the one shop in town that sells Swiss chocolate, or American pickles, or English Marmite. Go with the feeling; there's no shame in embracing your culinary birthright! That monthly trip to the German bakery or the local Irish pub is a chance to celebrate where you are from, raise a glass with some fellow expats and perhaps start a conversation with someone you've never met about the green, green grass of home.

★ Socialise

Being a location-independent freelancer doesn't have to be a silent meditation retreat. Co-working spaces are full of people in transit with ideas to share and inside knowledge of how to get the best out of being in a new country. Most co-working spaces offer regular social and networking sessions, or investigate meetups run by Facebook groups for digital nomads and expats; Meetup (www.meetup.com) is just one place to start looking for the next networking encounter.

★ Go on a date

Maybe you're spoken for, or part of a nomad couple. If not, travel is a great way to meet new people. Co-working networking sessions are a great way to expand your social circle, but don't be the office party middle manager who sees potential romance in every new employee. Dating apps or meeting people through courses and activities is usually a better bet. If nothing else, dating will help you see a city in a whole new light.

★ Taking a course

Being away from familiar comforts represents a rare chance to invest time in personal development. Learning the local language is a great place to start – and a great way to meet other people in the same position as you are – but you could study almost anything. As well as gaining a new skill, you'll gain a new sense of purpose, and meet other people who share the same interests.

Staying connected

Like an astronaut taking a space-walk, you became a digital nomad for the adventurous lifestyle, not to float off alone into the vast emptiness of space. Staying connected to home is an important step in keeping yourself grounded and maintaining key relationships with friends and family. Remember, no traveller is an island, even if you end up living on one!

© MATT MUNRO / LONELY PLANET

© CAIAIMAGE / TREVOR ADELINE / GETTY IMAGES

Thanks to modern tech, keeping in touch is easier than at any time in human history (pity the early explorers who were only able to send a message home once every few years, or the castaways sending messages home in a bottle). Email has almost totally superseded snail mail, and social media apps have made it possible to keep in touch almost every moment of every day.

However, there are some helpful ground rules for connecting with the folks back home. First and foremost is to keep communication personal. Instagram is fine for the edited version of your life; messages to friends and family are the place to share your thoughts and feelings and break down some of the isolation of being a stranger far from home.

SHARING DISPATCHES FROM THE ROAD

Everyone wants to show their trip in the best possible light to friends and family back home, but if every experience is amazing and every encounter so much deeper and more profound than experiences back home, your audience is going to start to lose interest. Here are some tips for sharing travel tales that will bring people along on your journey.

Share the reality
It's easy to edit your day and just share the positives, but friends and family are interested in the warts-and-all version of your life, not just the edited-for-Instagram highlights. Share the highs and the lows, and your support network will feel involved and ready to see you through the bad times as well as the good.

Be seen & heard
Texts, emails and posts have their place, but they're no substitute for face-to-face. Use video-calling apps like Skype, WhatsApp, Google Hangouts and Apple Facetime to keep in touch, and pick up the phone to let people know what's happening in your world.

Write personal messages
Your friends and family deserve the personal touch, so write individual messages rather than cc-ing everyone on chain messages or directing people to Facebook posts. And go old-school with a postcard occasionally, to remind people you're thinking of them.

Talk often
There's no need to speak every day or every week, but keeping in regular contact will put folks back home at ease. Check in before and after you move locations, and shout if you'll be out of contact for a while, so people don't think you've dropped off the map.

Show life not the sights
To bring the folks back home along on your trip, show them the everyday of the travel experience – where you're staying, what you're eating, the people you meet, how you're getting around.

It's not all about you
An endless feed of 'me, me, me' will cause anyone to turn off. Ensure there's give and take, and remember to ask about what's happening with people back home.

TOP TIP
'When sharing photographs of your trip, it's the details that make things personal. A snap of your feet showing the tan lines from your sandals, or a selfie with the old man on the harbour who sells grilled fish sandwiches and knows your daily order will give a much more vivid impression of your day-to-day life than endless shots of temples and tourist sights.'

Joe Bindloss, travel writer

10 GREAT APPS

FOR STAYING CONNECTED ON THE ROAD

You probably don't need an app to time the chicken on the barbecue, but keeping in touch with folks back home is where apps come into their own. Here are our communication essentials.

1 Instagram
www.instagram.com
For ease of use and immediacy, it's hard to beat the visual punch of Instagram. However, it doesn't always feel that personal, so don't make it your only mode of communication.

2 WhatsApp
www.whatsapp.com
Give and take is the beauty of WhatsApp. You and your friends and family can share experiences on a forum that includes just the people you want to connect with.

3 Facebook
www.facebook.com
An oldie but a goodie, if you don't mind surrendering some of your privacy, with endless tools that make it easy to broadcast your experiences to everyone you are connected with.

4 Skype
www.skype.com
The godfather of internet telephony, and still one of the most user-friendly interfaces for making free calls via the web. Transforms your mobile phone into a *Star Trek*-style communicator.

5 Viber
www.viber.com
Skype's closest challenger, offering free calls and messaging over the web, with the bonus of image and video sharing, and a paid-for service for calls to standard phones and mobiles.

6 Tripcast
www.tripcast.com
Share every step of your journey on an app that lets you post photos, tag locations and invite people along for the ride. Everything updates in real time, so people can follow your travels moment by moment.

7 Livetrekker
www.livetrekker.com
Create a multimedia diary of your trip, using pictures, video, audio and text to bring the journey to life for armchair travellers back home.

8 Rebtel
www.rebtel.com
Web-based calls rely on fast internet; Rebtel bypasses this by connecting international calls via local phone lines. You can buy destination-specific call bundles for many places around the world.

9 TripIt
www.tripit.com
As well as storing travel itinerary info, TripIt lets you share plans with people back home – perfect for nervous relations who want to keep track of exactly where you are.

10 Touchnote
www.touchnote.com
One for tech travellers who appreciate the value of something you can hold in your hand. Allows you to upload photos to be sent as postcards, usually for a lower cost than posting overseas by conventional mail.

LEARNING THE LINGO

The first rule of fitting in anywhere is communication. Even if all your digital business is with people back home, learning some of the local language will help with the logistics of running your business overseas, as well as making you feel more grounded and part of the local community.

Being in destination puts you in a unique position to learn a language through practical application – ie by talking to people, rather than staring at a whiteboard in a classroom. You'll come away with a much stronger grasp of syntax and grammar if you use a language every day, rather than just for an hour every Tuesday.

You could try learning online – there are hundreds of apps and sites that promise fast results with minimum effort – but you'll progress faster by talking to real people. Most nomad hangouts are well set up for language learning, with all sorts of long- and short-term courses slanted towards the international traveller, and learning a language can open up new opportunities for paid work, including online language teaching.

WHAT TO LOOK FOR FROM A LANGUAGE COURSE

Finding a course is usually easy in places where travellers gather. Check magazines and websites for travellers and expats, advertisements at local colleges and universities, or CourseFinders (www.coursefinders.com). Look for the following:

★ Small class sizes, or a good tutor-to-student ratio
★ Interactive learning, not just front-of-classroom instruction
★ Clear stages of development
★ Courses tailored to your needs
★ Good feedback from former students
★ Accreditation from international bodies

SHORTCUT APPS

There's no shame in turning to these tried and tested translation apps to learn the local phrase for 'where's the nearest wi-fi hotspot':

Google Translate
https://translate.google.com
As efficient as the online version, with handwriting recognition and a camera-based decoder perfect for translating signs and menus.

TripLingo
www.triplingo.com
Great for picking up the nuances of language, with alternative translations and slang. The basic version is free; a monthly fee unlocks the full potential.

iTranslate
www.itranslate.com
Fifty thousand iTunes users can't be wrong. The highly rated free version is filled with features, but the paid version includes a real-time voice translator.

TEN GREAT WAYS

TO OVERCOME LONELINESS

No matter how great your travel experiences, or how well your digital business is flourishing, or no man – or should that be nomad? – is an island. Here are some tricks for beating loneliness as you travel the information superhighway.

1 REMEMBER YOUR MOTIVATION

You went on the road for a reason, so focus on the opportunities that being a digital nomad brings as a way to beat the travel blues. Make a list of the things that motivated you to leave home, and the benefits you enjoy as a peripatetic professional, as a reminder of why you went on this journey.

2 TREAT YOURSELF

All work and no play is no fun for anyone. Reward yourself for all your hard work with little perks: treat meals, a day at the beach, spa treatments, a cinema trip. If the daily grind starts to wear you down, take a mini-break or stay in upmarket digs for couple of nights to recharge; you'll come back to your work routine refreshed and reinvigorated.

3 PLAN MICRO-ADVENTURES

Solitude always feels easier when you have a mission. Break up your work time with small adventures – wild swimming, forest treks, climbing to the temple on the hilltop, exploring the local area by moped – to keep things fresh and exciting.

© ILAN SHACHAM / GETTY IMAGES

4 LEARN SOMETHING NEW

Travel opens up all sorts of opportunities to develop as a person, whether that means learning a new language or taking your first scuba dive on a tropical reef. As well as helping you feel that things are moving forward, joining a course is a great way to meet fellow travellers with similar interests.

© EPICUREAN / GETTY IMAGES

5 RIDE THE ENDORPHIN EXPRESS

It's easy to let your exercise routine slide when you're away, and lack of exercise can lead to demotivation, lethargy and depression. Take the time to reward yourself with a trip to the gym, a swim or a run to fill your body with natural hormones that help you stay positive and motivated. Being outside can also give you a top-up dose of depression-beating Vitamin D.

6 TALK ABOUT IT

Talking to people you know and love is the perfect tonic if solitude starts to overwhelm. Nine times out of ten, friends and family would love to be in your shoes, and talking over the highs and lows can help put everything into perspective.

7 SOCIALISE

It sounds obvious, but many nomads get so focused on the mission that they forget to connect with the people around them. Join a club, go on a group trip, talk to the people sharing your co-working space, and you'll soon find you aren't as alone as you thought you were.

8 CONNECT WITH LOCALS

Fellow travellers aren't the only avenue for conversation. Engage with locals – shopkeepers, hotel staff, work contacts – and all sorts of social opportunities can arise. Even a chat about the weather can be enough to make you feel part of a community rather than a digital castaway, marooned with your laptop. For a novel way to meet local people, join a local-led tour at With Locals (www.withlocals.com).

9 SEEK OUT SOCIAL ACCOMMODATION

A rented apartment or hotel room grants maximum privacy and minimum interaction; many digital nomads prefer to stay in hostels or co-living spaces to meet fellow travellers and plug into social scenes. Bring interaction into your work environment, too – a co-working space will always mean more chances to chat than working alone in your room.

10 TRAVEL POSITIVE

Your body language can have a big effect on how you are perceived. If you walk around with a smile and a friendly manner, you are holding up a subliminal sign that you are someone positive to talk to. Conversely, walking around looking sullen and preoccupied may deter people who would otherwise love to chat.

Keeping healthy on the road

Getting ill is no fun. Getting ill when you are alone in an unfamiliar country far from home, with nobody to bring you a soothing mug of lemon tea, can be even worse. And unlike most workers, digital nomads work on a freelance basis, meaning a day off work is a day without pay – adding to the gloom of coming down with a bug.

Without your usual support network, you'll need to be extra diligent about keeping healthy, eating well, and taking care of yourself if you do get ill. As a starting point, pick up a copy of *Travelling Well* by Dr Deborah 'Deb' Mills, a comprehensive guide to everything you need to know about staying healthy while travelling, available online at www.thetraveldoctor.com.au.

Good hygiene

Poor hygiene is the cause of many illnesses that affect travellers. Foreign countries may have lower standards of hygiene than you are used to, particularly in food preparation. Be careful about what you eat and drink, and carry hand sanitizer or wash with soap and water before you eat. In the developing world, thoroughly wash fresh fruit or vegetables with purified water and, where possible, peel before you tuck in.

Stay hydrated

In hot climates and at altitude, your body will lose more water than normal, so stay hydrated. Travel medics recommend drinking eight glasses of water a day as a minimum – and that's good, old-fashioned H20 rather than diuretics such as coffee, fizzy drinks and alcohol. Stick to purified water, ideally using your own water bottle rather than adding to the world's plastic waste mountain, unless you want to play stomach bug roulette.

© MATT MUNRO / LONELY PLANET

Respect the sun

People who live in tropical climates go to great lengths to protect against the sun's harmful rays. Follow the old Australian adage 'Slip, Slop, Slap' – slip on a shirt, slop on some sunscreen, slap on a hat – and your skin will thank you for it. In many countries, covering up bare skin will also earn the respect of locals, who dress modestly for cultural and practical reasons.

Don't let the bedbugs bite

Though irritating, bedbugs are not a major health concern. Mosquitoes are the ones to watch. Malaria and dengue fever are just two serious diseases carried by these pesky insects, so take precautions to avoid being bitten, even if you're taking anti-malarial tablets. Sleep under a net, use a repellent containing diethyltoluamide (DEET), and wear light-coloured clothing to cover up bare skin at times when mosquitoes are on the prowl. Taking steps to avoid tick bites in rural areas is another top tip.

Get insured

The top-class medical treatment you get at home may not continue when on the road. Most of the world relies on pay-as-you-go healthcare, sometimes of variable quality, and the costs can be staggering – treating a broken leg can cost thousands of dollars, an air-ambulance rescue more than the deposit for a house. Always take out travel insurance with comprehensive health cover that includes emergency evacuation if a condition can't be treated locally.

Local meds

In many countries, medicines are available over the counter without prescription, but may not be stored safely, and may not be what they say they are. 'I strongly advise against buying local medicines,' says Dr Deb. 'Prices may be low but it's a false economy to buy drugs overseas – if you need medication you want to know you are getting the right stuff.' Fight the Fakes (www.fightthefakes.org) has more information.

Not every critter is cute

Feral dogs and cats are often adorably cute, and often infected with diseases including, potentially, rabies. 'It is a myth that you can just keep away from dogs and be safe from the risk of rabies,' warns Dr Deb. 'I've treated a host of patients who were bitten and did nothing more than wander about as a tourist.' Consider a rabies vaccination and seek urgent medical attention if bitten by any animal overseas. Monkeys are another common carrier, and can be aggressive towards humans, particularly over food.

TOP TIP

Dr Deb (www.thetraveldoctor.com.au) advises all travellers to follow these three key pieces of advice:

1. Get professional travel advice early, from doctors who have formal qualifications in travel health, and get all necessary vaccines – the diseases are much worse!

2. Carry a medical kit with clear instructions, and keep the hotline number for your travel insurance handy.

3. Get a full medical check-up before you go, including dental health.

HEALTHY EATING

When caught up in the excitement of a foreign country, it's easy to skip meals, overeat treat foods and forget everything you learned about following a balanced diet. Make sure the food you eat has a good mix of food groups and pack your diet with plenty of vegetables and fresh fruit (peeled or washed if you are worried about hygiene).

Food tips for travellers

One reason many of the world's cuisines are so delicious is that they are packed full of salt, sugar and oils. Local people stay slim through moderation and an active lifestyle; feasting on this culinary bounty day in and day out without keeping up activity levels can leave you feeling lethargic and tired in the short term, and worse in the long term.

Mix up oily dishes such as tacos and pizzas with salads, soups and fresh fruit, and monitor portion size – you don't have to finish a huge plateful just because that's how dinner was served. Choose something other than food as your go-to reward – a massage, exercise, a night at the cinema – and try to establish a healthy routine, rather than treating every meal as a special occasion just because you are away from home. Going vegetarian (even for just a few days a week) is another great way to cut out fats and maximise fibre.

Drink healthy

The motto 'all things in moderation' applies as strongly to drinking. If your goal is earning money while you travel, the expats you see drinking as soon as the sun hits the yardarm are probably not the lifestyle coaches to follow. Make alcohol something to enjoy at the end of a hard week of work, rather than a nightly pick-me-up, and your liver and bank balance will thank you.

Caffeine comes with the territory in the digital nomad world. Working all day in coffee shops and co-working spaces can mean drinking coffee by the bucketload. Mix up the flat whites with teas (don't forget green and herbal) plus juices and smoothies and you'll sleep better, stress less and work more productively. Remember, caffeine isn't a fix for being tired; sleep is.

© XSANDRA / GETTY IMAGES

© VLADISLAV NOSICK / 500PX

© FRANTICOO / SHUTTERSTOCK

Hygiene 101

Bugs in food and drink are the most common cause of illness amongst travellers. To avoid a bout of travellers' tummy, stick to food that you can see being freshly prepared in front of you, and avoid dishes that have been left sitting around at room temperature. Be cautious of seafood and undercooked meat and poultry, and stick to restaurants and food stalls that have lots of customers; quiet places are often quiet for a reason. Many travellers go vegetarian specifically to avoid the risks associated with meat and fish.

Never drink tap water unless you are sure it is safe; even brushing your teeth with water from the tap can be enough to get a bug. Stick to bottled purified water or, even better, refill your own water bottle and reduce plastic waste. Be careful with salads – they may have been washed in contaminated water – and avoid ice unless you are certain it was made with purified water. Ice cream is also a no-no unless you are sure it has never been defrosted and refrozen.

Sexual health

We're all adults here; travel romances are part of travel, and plenty of lifelong relationships have started with a chance encounter in a backpacker bar. With inhibitions lowered, casual sexual encounters are common, both with fellow travellers and locals. But it pays to take steps to avoid sexually transmitted diseases (STDs).

'Beware of alcohol,' warns Dr Deb. 'It destroys people's good intentions about practising safe sex, and many STDs are becoming resistant to antibiotics.' Carry contraception from home, as locally made products may not be of the same standard – poorly made condoms can split, increasing the risk of pregnancy and STDs. Note that the morning-after pill is only available in certain countries, and an unwanted pregnancy could bring a sudden end to your trip.

Instances of serious diseases like HIV, gonorrhoea, syphilis and hepatitis B and C may be high in developing countries. Remember, too, that sexual contact is not the only way to contract an STD. These diseases can also be spread by blood transfusions, tattooing and reused hypodermic needles – to reduce the risks, always seek out medical establishments that conform to international standards.

EXERCISE YOUR WAY HEALTHY

The digital nomad lifestyle can carry plenty of stress about where the next pay check is coming from. Few things are as good for your physical and mental health as exercise that raises the heart rate for 30 minutes or more; get active and you'll feel happier, healthier and ready to take on new challenges.

Join a gym

Travelling with a set of barbells is probably going too far, but joining a local gym can be a good option – and it's an easy way to meet local people. In destinations popular with travellers, gyms may have temporary memberships for transient visitors – ask fellow remote workers for recommendations. Mid-range and high-end hotels frequently have some kind of fitness centre with machines and free-weights; and co-work spaces with gyms are also becoming easier to find.

Swim free

You can wild swim almost anywhere you find water, though it pays to check the currents and hygiene levels before you dive in. If you can't find clean water, swimming pools are the safe option, though you may need to follow the local etiquette on swimwear; many countries insist on skimpy trunks and tight bathing suits. If your budget doesn't stretch to a hotel with a pool, many upmarket hotels will let non-guests use their facilities for a fee.

Run, skip & jump

There's always the *Rocky IV* approach: exercising using whatever tools nature can provide. Running is possible almost anywhere, though you might have to adjust your schedule to avoid tropical heat. Consider contacting a local running club – the Hash House Harriers have regular meets all over the world where expats get together for a social trot (search online for 'hash house harriers' and the name of your city). Although it might seem old fashioned, a skipping rope is the exercise machine you can fit into a carry-on bag.

Stretch out

Yoga is the ultimate portable exercise regime. It takes minimal space, needs minimal equipment and will leave you feeling refreshed and invigorated and ready for whatever travel throws at you. Not that bendy? Try *tai chi quan*; every day in China, millions of people of all ages flock to parks and public spaces to start the day with an activity that relaxes both body and mind.

TOP TIP

'Local swimming pools and gyms can be great places to unwind – but are also easy places to pick up a fungal or viral infection, particularly from the floor of the shower. Nasties you could pick up range from small but irritating infections such as verrucas to dangerous methicillin-resistant Staphylococcus. Wear flip-flops to reduce the risks.'
Joe Bindloss, travel writer,
www.bindloss.co.uk

Personal Safety

Statistically, travel has never been safer, despite news reports to the contrary. Easy access to information helps travellers stay away from danger, and in general, safety standards are increasing across the world.

Taking out comprehensive travel insurance is one of the most important things you can do to stay safe on the road, and it also pays to respect local laws, particularly when it comes to drugs. If you get arrested for breaking the law in another country, all your embassy may be able to do is help you find a local lawyer.

CRIME

Crime is the biggest fear for most travellers, and a particular worry for digital nomads trying to run a business from their laptop.

★ Keep your precious tech out of sight when not in use, and never leave laptops or phones unattended in cafes and co-working spaces.

★ Don't walk around with expensive cameras, sunglasses or jewellery on prominent display.

★ Make life hard for pickpockets – don't put your phone or wallet in your back pocket, and keep your bag in sight at all times.

★ Never leave anything of value in a car, especially overnight, and keep the doors locked when you are stationary.

★ Only stay in hotels where you can lock the doors and windows securely from the inside; avoid ground floor rooms, which are easier to break into.

★ Consider fire safety – check evacuation routes and don't stay in a room with bars over the windows.

★ Lock away valuables in a hotel safe or a locked bag in your room.

★ Carry photocopies of all your important documents – passports, driving licences, bank cards – and send email scans to yourself so you have a backup.

★ Take extra care at ATMs, and never let a vendor take your card out of your sight.

★ Avoid walking down empty streets, in the daytime as well as at night.

★ Take extra care if you have been drinking (drop your bag off where you are staying before you head out).

★ Avoid cybercrime – see our tips for Tech-Safe Travel (p77).

★ If you are a victim of crime, get a report from the local police to claim on your insurance.

★ If you are robbed, give thieves what they want – valuables can be replaced, you can't.

★ Be wary of over-friendly strangers who insist on starting up a conversation; this is often the start of a scam.

★ Don't accept drinks or food from strangers; drugging is a risk in some countries.

★ Watch out for scams; touts will try to steer you towards places that pay a commission, taxi meters are frequently 'broken', and deals that sound too good to be true invariably are.

TRANSPORT SAFETY

Transport overseas is a common cause of anxiety for travellers, but the risks are often lower than many people imagine, though travel by road or by boat can be much more dangerous than flying.

★ When flying, stick to reputable airlines and watch out for carriers on international banned lists – the Aviation Safety Network (www.aviation-safety.net) has safety reports on most airlines.

★ Be wary of smaller airlines; they can go bankrupt at short notice, and travel insurance may not cover you for airline failure.

★ Consider the weather – there are additional risks to flying during the rainy season or cold conditions in winter.

★ Always leave a time buffer between domestic and international flights in case of delays, particularly if the flights are on separate tickets.

★ When hiring a vehicle overseas, take out as much insurance cover as you can get; insurance excesses can be crippling.

★ If you hire any vehicle, make sure that you are insured for damage to the vehicle and for health costs and damage if you hit someone else.

★ Be cautious of leaving your passport as security for renting a moped or motorcycle; companies operating this way rarely provide adequate insurance.

★ Follow local road rules, including speed limits and unwritten 'rules' such as always giving way to the largest vehicle.

★ Make sure your driving licence is valid (an international driving licence may be required) and carry it with you at all times.

★ Consider hiring a car and driver so you don't have to worry about adjusting to the local driving conditions.

★ Avoid bus travel at night – drivers often take advantage of empty roads to drive at even more terrifying speeds.

★ Safety standards for travel by boat can be woeful – check out safety standards of local operators and stay close to emergency exits or on deck.

★ Arrive during daylight hours, and consider pre-booking transport to your accommodation, to avoid having to navigate unfamiliar streets in the dark.

★ Carry the business card of where you are staying so you can show it to a taxi driver if you get lost.

★ If you plan to go trekking or travel off the beaten track, let someone know when you are leaving and when you intend to be back.

TERRORISM & POLITICAL UNREST

If you believe tabloid newspapers, the world is deadly and the only safe option is to stay at home. In reality, the risk of being caught up in terrorism or political unrest overseas is pretty small, especially if you avoid unstable areas.

★ Always check government travel advisories before you travel – government departments, such as the British Foreign & Commonwealth Office (www.gov.uk/foreign-travel-advice) and US State Department (http://travel.state.gov) publish regular updates to countries around the world.

★ Check local news sources for reports on violence and unrest, and areas to avoid; these may be more up-to-date than government advisories.

★ Avoid travelling to countries or regions with an 'avoid-all-travel' warning as you may not be covered by your travel insurance.

★ Stay away from political rallies, protests and demonstrations; they can turn violent with little warning.

★ Be cautious when travelling during elections, or during religious holidays in countries with intercommunal tensions.

★ Be careful in large crowds; to avoid being crushed, stay on your feet, use your arms to create breathing space and work your way to the edge of the crowd.

★ Avoid travel during public strikes – protesters often target buses, trains and airports, and drivers flouting travels bans are sometimes attacked.

★ Be vigilant in places popular with international tourists and in public markets; both are possible targets for terrorist attacks.

SPECIAL CONSIDERATIONS FOR WOMEN & LGBT TRAVELLERS

It is an unfortunate reality that women and LGBT travellers face additional risks from sexual harassment and homophobia.

★ If someone encroaches on your personal space, complain loudly; pests are often deterred by the negative attention.

★ Never get into a taxi if there is someone else inside apart from the driver; it's often safer to call for a taxi rather than hailing a cab in the street.

★ Check local laws and attitudes towards same-sex relationships before you travel; in some countries, same-sex couples are at risk of arrest or violence.

★ Follow the lead of locals on appropriate clothing, particularly away from cosmopolitan cities.

SIX APPS FOR STAYING SAFE

Your mobile phone is a helpful ally when it comes to staying safe overseas. As well as making emergency calls, you can download all sorts of apps to make your trip trouble-free. Enter local emergency phone numbers into your address book, get a local SIM (or enable roaming on your home account) and carry a portable battery power block so your phone is always charged and ready for action.

BSafe (www.getbsafe.com)

Creates a network of emergency contacts and automatically notifies them in an emergency, or if you hit a panic button. A voice-activated alarm can trigger an audio recording of whatever's happening and send it to your contacts.

ICE – In Case of Emergency (Sylvain Lagache)

A log of medical conditions and insurance company/doctor contract details placed on your lock screen, accessible even if your phone is locked.

CDC Apps (www.cdc.gov)

Just one of many useful CDC apps, Travwell compiles trip-specific travel health advice (including local emergency numbers), records your meds/jabs, and works online and offline.

CityMapper (www.citymapper.com)

Safe transport advice, including ride-hailing apps, in many cities worldwide.

SmartTraveler (http://travel.state.gov)

The latest US government travel advisories compiled into a handy database.

Offline Survival Manual (Ligi)

This digital handbook has reams of advice on survival skills, including building shelters, recognising poisonous plants and field medicine.

Planning for your return

At the start of the journey, it's easy to imagine being a digital nomad forever, but a lot can happen on life's highway. You might find yourself missing the friends and stability of home. You might run out of cash. You might meet someone new and fall in love. There are a million different reasons why you might decide you've come to the end of the road, so it pays to have a plan in place for how you are going to exit the peripatetic life.

Money matters

Just as that nest egg came in handy when you started as a digital nomad, you'll need a financial buffer to reintegrate into life back home. Costs are likely to be higher than when you went away, so make your last nomad base somewhere super-cheap with minimal distractions, so you can work longer, be more productive, and spend less of the money you'll need to rebuild at home.

Don't underestimate the time this will take. Saving up enough for a stress-free return could be a three-month, six-month or year-long enterprise, without some of the lifestyle perks you may have become accustomed to. Approach this as a business decision, and stay focused on the goal of achieving a home lifestyle that's at least as rewarding as your life while travelling.

The cost of living

Think ahead about ways to keep costs down until you're in a financially stable position. Finding a job before you fly home is obviously the ideal, but this can take time; you might need to become a non-nomadic digital freelancer while you look for something permanent. As well as facing higher living costs, you'll have taxes to pay and red tape to unravel – be realistic about how much money you'll need.

Accommodation is likely to be the biggest cost, so think of steps you can take to keep overheads down. Could you couch-surf, or move in with relatives while you look for work? A room in a house-share will be cheaper than renting a whole apartment, with the added bonus of people to talk to as you adjust to a world where you can't cure boredom by just moving on.

Back to work

Think about how to describe your time as a digital nomad in job interviews. Presenting it in terms of skills acquired, lessons learned and wisdom gained could put you ahead of those on a conventional career path. 'Be prepared to answer questions about your time abroad,' advises Laura Holden, Communications Executive at Reed Online (www.reedglobal.com). 'Articulate what you gained from the experience and how you can use your skills to benefit your new employer. It's also important to think carefully about why you want to make the transition from "digital nomad" to a more traditional stand-still career. Most employers will want to have reassurance that you're capable of working in this kind of environment, and that you won't get itchy feet anytime soon.'

TOP TIP

'Returning to settled life can be a jolt to the system, so approach coming home with the same sense of focus as when you went on the road. Make sure you have enough funds to support yourself and a clear plan for where to stay and how to go about making money when you get home.'

Joe Bindloss, travel writer, www.bindloss.co.uk

Job-search tips

Keep your resume with you on the road and keep it up to date with new skills and achievements as you go, and use your network to investigate job opportunities before you head home

Companies you have freelanced for may have more substantial opportunities for you once you get home, so don't be afraid to ask. Use the full range of online job-hunting tools – industry noticeboards, Linkedin (www.linkedin.com), job sites such as Reed, Indeed (www.indeed.com), CareerBuilder (www.careerbuilder.com) and Monster (www.monster.com) – and make sure your online and social media presence makes it clear that you are available and looking for work.

Reintegrating

For the first couple of weeks, friends and family will love to hear about your travels and adventures, but be assured that the novelty will wear off. Don't let the celebrity vibe of being the returning prodigal son (or daughter) go to your head. Remember that what everyone else has been doing deserves just as much airtime as your tale of the time you climbed Kilimanjaro.

Be ready for the fact that some relationships may not have stood the test of time. Some people will have moved on, or started a new life elsewhere. Unless you are very lucky, the support network you left behind will not be the same support network you come home to, so be ready to use the skills you honed networking at nomad meetups to strike up new friendships and business relationships.

TOP DESTINATIONS FOR DIGITAL NOMADS

Practicalities

✈ Ngurah Rai International Airport, Denpasar

LGBT-friendly
Yes

🧳 Fast ferries connect Bali to Lombok, Java and the Gili Islands.

📅 April through June sees dry days and manageable temperatures in Bali, but prices climb in August. The rainy season from September to March offers plenty of reasons to stay indoors in your co-working space; some decamp to drier parts of the world for the rainy months.

$ From US$1000 per month

Canggu, Bali, Indonesia

The destination that put being a digital nomad on the map, Canggu is still top of the bucket list for travelling freelancers who insist on warm weather, fast internet, easy access to coconuts and a co-working space with a pool. Add in plenty of cheap villa accommodation, great food and an easy-going pace of life firmly oriented towards the visiting traveller and it's easy to see the appeal.

It was visiting surfers who first hit on the idea of remote working from Bali while enjoying the beach breaks. Canggu rose to the occasion, serving up a full platter of remote working facilities and abundant ways to fill downtime at nearby Kuta, Seminyak and Ubud. Canggu is certainly one of the world's most relaxing workplaces, with opportunities for pre-work yoga and after-office surfing before settling down to a swordfish supper at Jimbaran Beach.

Nevertheless, the endless focus on the visitor leaves some digital nomads aching for a little more culture and local character. Ubud, in the rice-terraced uplands to the east, is fast stealing Canggu's thunder as a more authentic, less hedonistic place to do business. With easy transport links, plenty of nomads split their time between Ubud and Canggu – in lifestyle terms, it's a bit like having a house in the hills and a condo on the coast.

Pros & cons

GREAT FOR:
★ Social life
★ Leisure activities
★ Networking opportunities
★ Food and coffee shops
★ Cheap digs

NOT SO GREAT FOR:
★ Authentic local culture
★ Peace and quiet
★ Ways to escape
★ Short-notice availability in co-working spaces
★ Rainy days

CO-WORKING SPACES

* A legendary spot for remote workers, **Dojo Bali** (www.dojobali.org) offers monthly packages and day passes, with multiple connections via multiple ISPs, so you can be confident your internet access won't go down. There's a cafe and a pool, it's minutes from Echo Beach, and it's open 24/7.
* Digital nomads rate the calm environment and ergonomic seating at **Outpost Canggu** (www.destinationoutpost.co/location/canggu) as being particularly conducive to productivity. As with other Canggu spaces, there's air-con, a cafe and a pool, and members have access to reliable high-speed connections 24 hours a day. It also offers co-living space.

LIVING ARRANGEMENTS

Hotels, hostels and beach resorts abound, but most digital nomads prefer to rent a villa or *kos* (like a smaller apartment). Try the Facebook groups **Bali Canggu Housing & Accommodation** (www.facebook.com/groups/1380848555535084) and **Canggu Community House** (www.facebook.com/groups/746999628699757) for listings. Cheap, healthy food can be found everywhere for penny prices. Don't miss the island's spectacular street food – coconut-infused *sate lilit* (grilled meat skewers) is a particular favourite – and delicious seafood, served fresh on the beach. Travel by bus, *bemo* (minivan) or taxi or rent a scooter to get around.

©JOYFULL / SHUTTERSTOCK

Previous page: Canggu beach; Left: Sunrise at Canggu; Opposite: Rice terraces at Tegallalang.

NETWORKING

★ Digital Nomads Bali
(www.facebook.com/groups/553237938183702)
★ Canggu Entrepreneurs & Digital Nomads
(www.facebook.com/groups/1189122534499703)
★ Bali Digital Nomads
(www.facebook.com/groups/balidigitalnomads)

PRE-DEPARTURE READING

* Lonely Planet's *Bali, Lombok & Nusa Tenggara* guidebook

* *A House in Bali* by Colin McPhee

* *Love and Death in Bali* by Vicky Baum

* *A Little Bit One O'clock: Living with a Balinese Family* by William Ingram

INTERNET SPEEDS

Fast, and getting faster, but it depends on the location; expect download speeds of 2 Mbps via cafe wi-fi, but a hundred times that in co-working spaces, which should also have back-up generators to keep you working through Bali's periodic power outages.

Ways to unwind

Surf the breaks of Bali's southwest coast – serious surfers rate Ulu Watu, Padang Padang, Balangan and other strips to the south over the popular beginners' breaks at Kuta, Seminyak and Legian.

—

Day trip to Ubud – escape the beach resort scene for Bali's cultural capital, to wander in green, tropical hills, take in traditional dance shows and relax with a spa session or a yoga class.

—

Island-hop to Nusa Lembongan – find the Bali you imagined on this laid-back island, with good surfing, excellent diving, and cheap rooms by the beach.

© EDMUND LOWE PHOTOGRAPHY / SHUTTERSTOCK

Practicalities

✈ Lisbon Portela Airport, Lisbon

LGBT-friendly
Yes

🧳 Trains and buses connect to Lisbon from across Europe.

📅 Spring (March–May) and autumn (September–August) are optimum, with balmy temperatures and quieter streets; the incendiary summer (June–September) sees Lisbon mobbed by tourists. Many nomads relocate during the cold and quiet winter.

$ From €1000 per month

Lisbon, Portugal

The Portuguese capital has its eye on becoming Silicon Valley on the Tagus River, and Google is just one tech big-hitter to set up a base here, ensuring ready opportunities for developers. With the big city location, Lisbon appeals to digital nomads who come to work as much as play, though there's no shortage of great, affordable places to eat, drink and party for when the mood takes you.

Pros & cons

GREAT FOR:
★ Sense of community
★ Tech opportunities
★ Cheap, tasty food
★ Warm weather
★ High quality of life

NOT SO GREAT FOR:
★ Peace at night
★ Lack of crowding
★ Accommodation prices
★ Variety
★ Affordable flights to other countries

What nomads love best about Lisbon is the sense of community among freelancers. The Lisbon Digital Nomads Facebook group (www.facebook.com/groups/532696873566509) has nearly 11,000 members, and arranges weekly meetups for networking, socialising, eating, and just unwinding with a cold *cerveja* or a glass of *ginjinha* (cherry liqueur). Many co-working spaces have co-living accommodation and almost all arrange meetups.

Then there's the lifestyle. Despite its technological aspirations, Lisbon is one of Europe's most human-friendly capital cities, sprawling in a tangle of cobblestone streets over seven historic hills, and dotted with grand Pombaline architecture. Relaxed drinking laws mean that sleepy backstreets come alive at nightfall and fill with activity till the early morning hours, and by day, cafes with fast wi-fi serve dainty cups of *bica* (espresso coffee) to Lisbonites on the go.

CO-WORKING SPACES

* Space to think is the big appeal of **Heden** (www.heden.co), tucked into a busy square in Graça. Co-working spaces popular with devs share a site with artists' studios and a venue for talks and events, ensuring lots of creative crossover.
* Some co-working spaces can feel a bit like an Ikea showroom, but **Workhub Lisboa** (www.workhub.pt) has a gorgeous location in the old Abel Pereira da Fonseca wine warehouse, in the up-and-coming neighbourhood of Poco do Bispo. The internet connection is lightning fast and there's a casual lounge space, or desks and private offices rented by the month.

LIVING ARRANGEMENTS

Hotels and guesthouses are everywhere but most digital nomads opt for rented apartments and rooms or co-living accommodation – conveniently attached to many of the city's co-working spaces. Many find accommodation through Airbnb, but with the demand from tourists, it's often easier to find a room through people you meet via digital nomad meetups or through Facebook groups. Get around by city bus and tram and eat inexpensively at local *tascas* – family-run restaurants serving cheap *pratos do dia* (daily specials) that change through the week depending on what the owners have in the kitchen.

© RADU BERCAN / SHUTTERSTOCK

Previous page: Bica funicular; Left: Mercado da Ribiera; Opposite: Museu de Arte, Arquitetura e Tecnologia.

NETWORKING

* DigitalNomads.pt (www.digitalnomads.pt)
* Lisbon Digital Nomads (www.facebook.com/lisbondigitalnomads)
* Lisbon Digital Nomads Public Group (www.facebook.com/groups/532696873566509)

PRE-DEPARTURE READING

★

Lonely Planet's *Portugal* and *Pocket Lisbon* guidebooks

✳

Last Train to Lisbon by Pascal Mercier

✳

The Year of the Death of Ricardo Reis by José Saramago

✳

A Small Death in Lisbon by Robert Wilson

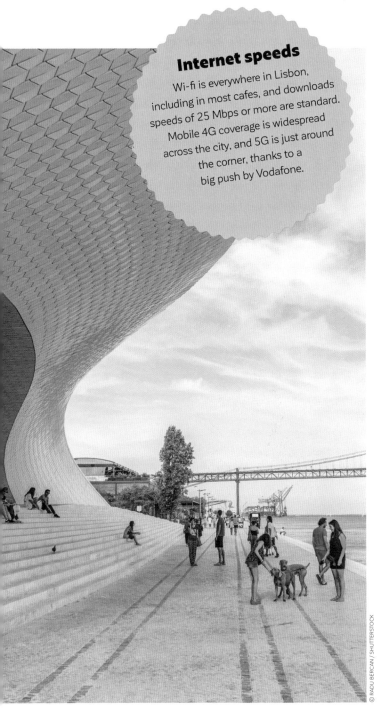

Internet speeds

Wi-fi is everywhere in Lisbon, including in most cafes, and downloads speeds of 25 Mbps or more are standard. Mobile 4G coverage is widespread across the city, and 5G is just around the corner, thanks to a big push by Vodafone.

Ways to unwind

Spend all night (and possibly some of the next morning) at a street party in Cais do Sodré or Bairro Alto – the Feast of St Anthony (Sardine Festival) on 12 June is one of Portugal's biggest public shindigs.

—

Escape the city crush to surf, splash or sunbathe at Costa de Caparica, Nazarè or Peniche, all within an hour and a half of downtown and accessible by local bus.

—

Soak up some chlorophyll in the green bower of Parque Florestal de Monsanto, a replanted forest sprawling along the city fringes, crisscrossed by hiking trails and dotted with lookouts with grand city views.

© RADU BERCAN / SHUTTERSTOCK

Practicalities

✈ Tan Son Nhat International, Ho Chi Minh City

LGBT-friendly
Yes

💼 Trains zip to Ho Chi Minh City from northern Vietnam while buses run to Phnom Penh in Cambodia.

📅 December to March is southern Vietnam's dry season, but it's super hot and everything goes into chaotic overdrive for the Tet Festival (January or February). The May-to-September rainy season brings high humidity, and starts with a blast of brutal heat.

$ From US$900 per month

Ho Chi Minh City, Vietnam

While Hanoi rocks, Ho Chi Minh City is rolling into the 21st century on a wave of tech development. Skyscrapers are shooting up, tech start-ups are appearing on every corner, and Richard Branson described the city as the next Silicon Valley, thanks to its highly motivated, highly educated tech workforce. There's even a self-styled Saigon Silicon City, under construction in District 9 in the eastern suburbs.

For digital nomads, the city serves up delicious street food, inexpensive accommodation and easy-to-find high-speed internet connections, plus a big-city vibe that appeals to remote workers who want easy access to everything 24 hours a day. However, many co-working spaces are as popular with local freelancers as visiting nomads, and you won't find the same sense of community as in more popular expat hubs, such as Chiang Mai or Canggu.

Those who love HCMC, love it for its energy and enthusiasm, its start-up mentality, and its design-oriented coffee shops serving full-bodied French-style coffee. On the flip side, the motorcycle traffic jams, air pollution and tropical heat can take some getting used to. When the city closes in, nomads retreat to the calmer surroundings of the Mekong Delta and such laid-back hangouts as Phu Quoc Island, with its beaches, diving and rainforest greenery.

Pros & cons

GREAT FOR:
★ Amazing food
★ Low cost of living
★ Plenty of culture
★ Can-do attitude
★ Coffee shops

NOT SO GREAT FOR:
★ Overcrowding
★ Pollution
★ Street crime
★ Traffic
★ Sense of community

CO-WORKING SPACES

★ Easily the best-loved co-working space in Ho Chi Minh, **Dreamplex** (www.dreamplex.co) has a District 1 location (in fact two of them, plus two more in Binh Thanh District), fast internet access and a no-nonsense business vibe that appeals to nomads who like to get their heads down to work.

★ For a more social vibe, **Spiced CoWorking** (www.start-saigon.com) is set in an area full of rooms for rent in District 2, and it hosts regular networking lunches and social gatherings, as well as offering its own co-living accommodation and a pool.

LIVING ARRANGEMENTS

Most remote workers base themselves centrally in Districts 1 and 3, while more established expats gravitate towards Districts 2 and 7. Rented apartments are the mainstay of nomad accommodation but central locations can be expensive; many transient workers prefer cheaper rooms in shared houses, though this can mean working in coffee shops and co-working spaces for relative peace and quiet. Then again, with Vietnam's fabulous street food, you'll want to eat out as often as possible. To get around, Uber and Grab offer a cheap alternative to local taxis, or do as locals do and jump on a motorcycle taxi.

© JINDOWIN / SHUTTERSTOCK

Previous page: Ho Chi Minh City; Left: Bai Sao beach, Phu Quoc; Opposite: Ho Chi Minh City skyline.

NETWORKING

★ Saigon Digital Nomads
(www.facebook.com/groups/saigonnomads)
★ Expats in Ho Chi Minh City
(www.facebook.com/groups/expatshcmc)
★ Ho Chi Minh City Expats
(www.facebook.com/HCMCExpats)

PRE-DEPARTURE READING

★
Lonely Planet's
Vietnam guidebook
★
The Quiet American
by Graham Greene
★
Saigon: An Epic Novel of Vietnam
by Anthony Grey
★
The Sympathizer: A Novel
by Viet Thanh Nguyen

INTERNET SPEEDS

High-speed internet is easy to find in Ho Chi Minh City, thanks to heavy investment from Singapore, and download speeds of 25 Mbps are common. Promised free city-wide wi-fi has yet to materialise, but you'll find inexpensive local SIMs for 4G mobile coverage.

Ways to unwind

Get down in Chinatown – the district of Cholon, 5km southwest of the centre, offers fabulous Chinese flavours, mercantile bustle and ornate pagodas spilling out of hidden courtyards.

—

Take a Delta tour – the green, rice-paddy-covered wetlands of the Mekong Delta are ripe for exploration; on organised tours, or independently by rented motorcycle, bus and boat.

—

Weekend break on the beach at Phu Quoc – VietJet Air and Jetstar offer cheap transfers to the island airstrip, putting Phu Quoc's beaches, beach bars and national park within easy reach.

Practicalities

✈ José María Córdova International Airport, Medellín

LGBT-friendly
Yes

🧳 Buses travel all over the country and to Colombia's borders from the two bus stations in Medellín.

📅 Medellín has a warm but moderate climate year-round, and the only significant variation is the amount of rain, with more showers than usual from April to May and September to November. Many resident expats live happily without air-conditioning or heating.

$ From US$1100 per month

Medellín, Colombia

Colombia has moved mountains to shake off its narco reputation, and Medellín is at the forefront of this national reinvention, picking up a string of awards for its innovative civic projects and commitment to sustainable urban development. Colombia's second city is also blessed with a temperate climate and a valley location that prevents the city from becoming too large and unmanageable.

Many of Medellín's growing population of digital nomads were lured south from North America by the city's low cost of living, good weather and solid infrastructure for remote working – from widespread wi-fi to a burgeoning coffee-shop culture. Medellín also has a good support network for new arrivals, with numerous digital nomad groups arranging regular social events. The scene started small in Medellín, but the city has a growing buzz, and it's fast becoming one of the top nomad stops in the Americas.

On top of this, you get culture, hospitable locals and great food and nightlife. Being in a similar time zone to the United States also doesn't hurt, particularly for nomads with stateside clients. However, to get the best out of living in Medellín, you'll need to speak good Spanish, something that will also open doors when networking with other entrepreneurs.

Pros & cons

GREAT FOR:
★ Year-round good weather
★ Low cost of living
★ Sharing a timezone with the US
★ Friendly people
★ Cheap public transport

NOT SO GREAT FOR:
★ Traffic
★ Pollution
★ Extending your visa
★ Non-Spanish speakers
★ Petty crime

CO-WORKING SPACES

★ For accommodation, co-working space, food, brews and everything else you need under one roof, Selina (www.selina.com/colombia/medellin) is a good starting point, with a handy El Poblado location.

★ Another space with a strong community ethos is Siembra Coworking/Ofizen (www.siembracoworking.com) in El Poblado, with regular quizzes, workshops, networking nights and free beer Fridays.

★ Nomads with a strong business focus rate Tinkko (www.tinkko.com), set on the 15th floor of a high-rise in the business district; it's a great place to work with a view, and there are proper meeting rooms for start-ups that are going places.

LIVING ARRANGEMENTS

Most nomads opt for rooms in shared apartments or rented apartments, which tends to mean living in the suburbs rather than the busy centre. Prices fall if you skip the touristy and central El Poblado neighbourhood for quieter areas, such as Ciudad del Rio, Estadio, Floresta and Laureles. If you speak good Spanish, the site Comparto Apto (www.compartoapto.com) can put you in touch with local landlords with rooms and apartments for rent. For food, graze the streets for *bandeja paisa* (meat, beans, rice and sides), arepas (stuffed cornflour cakes) and empanadas (Colombian pasties) and get around by local taxis, city buses and the Metro.

© SUNSINGER / SHUTTERSTOCK

Previous page: Medellín from the Parque Arvi cable car; Left: Botero Plaza; Opposite: Guatapé.

NETWORKING

★ Digital Nomads Medellín (www.facebook.com/groups/digitalnomadsmedellin)
★ Medellín Entrepreneurs Society (www.facebook.com/groups/MedellinEntrepreneursSociety)
★ Medellín Digital Nomads (www.facebook.com/groups/1527870354167112)

PRE-DEPARTURE READING

★

Lonely Planet's
Colombia guidebook

★

100 Years of Solitude
by Gabriel García
Márquez

★

Delirio by Laura Restrepo

★

*The Sound of
Things Falling*
by Juan Gabriel Vásquez

INTERNET SPEEDS

The average download speed via wi-fi is 10 Mbps, which is slower than in some nomad hubs, but faster connections are easy to find. Colombia has also been rolling out 4G coverage for several years, with decent access in urban areas.

Ways to unwind

Ride the cable car to Parque Arvi – this forested reserve beyond the city limits has pre-Hispanic ruins and plentiful wildlife; its walking trails (busy at weekends) offer peaceful respite from the city.

—

Climb Piedra El Peñol – climb 600 steps up this granite massif near Guatapé town (a two-hour bus ride from Medellín) for stunning views over deep-blue artificial lakes.

—

Seek out the perfect cup of Joe – Colombia's Unesco-listed coffee country is a few hours south of Medellín. Manizales is the gateway to historic coffee-estate haciendas, plantation tours and birding in Río Blanco Reserva Natural.

© SORIN RECHITAN / EYEEM / GETTY IMAGES

Practicalities

✈ Shota Rustaveli Tbilisi International Airport, Tbilisi

LGBT-friendly
No

💼 *Marshrutka* minibuses and trains buzz around Georgia and into Armenia, Azerbaijan and Turkey. To avoid crossing breakaway republic Abkhazia, most people fly to Russia.

📅 Spring (April to June) and autumn (September to October) are the most pleasant times to be here, avoiding the hot, muggy summer and cold, damp winter. But with a year of visa-free travel, many nomads stay 12 months and watch the changing seasons.

$ From US$900 per month

Tbilisi, Georgia

Former Soviet republics don't tend to feature high on nomad bucket lists, but Georgia is a notable exception. Culturally, the country looks towards Asia as much as Russia, and escape from the Soviets in 1991 kickstarted a process of reinvention that hasn't stopped yet. Capital Tbilisi hums with energy, with fast wi-fi available across the city and a remarkably easy-going pace of life.

Although the local cafe scene leans more towards old-fashioned tables on the pavement than the sleek hangouts more commonly associated with digital nomad culture, the combination of modern tech infrastructure and old-world charm is an enticing package for nomads who like a bit of nostalgia with their high-speed web connections. Picking up a smattering of spoken Georgian will ease your passage into the Tbilisi way of life.

A low cost of living is matched by a comfortable quality of life, and a liberal visa regime – with free, visa-free travel for a year for most nationalities – means you won't have to bother about such inconveniences as making a visa run across the border. What you won't find is quite the same level of networking and support as in more-established nomad hubs. No matter; the food and wine, produced here for nearly 8000 years, provides ample compensation.

Pros & cons

GREAT FOR:
★ Visa-free travel
★ Low cost of living
★ Great food
★ The birthplace of wine
★ Fast internet

NOT SO GREAT FOR:
★ Networking
★ Co-working infrastructure
★ Traffic
★ Bureaucracy
★ Urban care

CO-WORKING SPACES

★ With a prime location in the fashionable Fabrika development (a Soviet-era sewing factory reinvented as a hub for cafes, bars, concepts shops and the arts), Impact Hub Tbilisi (https://tbilisi.impacthub.net) is a nomad favourite, with events and meetups, fast web access and a bohemian lifestyle right on the doorstep.

★ Set amid the greenery in Vake Park, Mediathek (www.mediatheka.ge) is a public library with fast wi-fi and plenty of quiet desk spaces for working. A minimal annual fee covers the use of all facilities; there are similarly calm, modernist branches at Varketili and in Veterans Park in Nadzaladevi.

LIVING ARRANGEMENTS

Airbnb should be your first port of call when looking for a room or apartment to rent in Tbilisi. Downtown accommodation is expensive, so be ready to set up in the suburbs. Just outside the centre, the gentrifying districts of Vake and Avlabari are on the up and up. Be warned that many apartments have minimal heating; bring warm clothes for winter. For food, dine cheaply on *mtsvadi* (kebabs), *khachapuri* (cheese-stuffed bread) and *khinkali* (dumplings) at local restaurants. Getting around is easy by *marshrutka*, taxi, or local taxi-hailing app Yandex.Taxi (https://taxi.yandex.ru).

© ANNA BOGUSH / ALAMY STOCK PHOTO

Previous page: Narikala Fortress; Left: Downtown Tbilisi; Opposite: Cafe co-working at Fabrika.

NETWORKING

★ Tbilisi Digital Nomads (https://z-m-www.facebook.com/groups/tbilisidigitalnomad)
★ Tbilisi Expats Community (www.facebook.com/TbilisiExpatsCommunity)
★ Expats in Tbilisi (www.facebook.com/groups/310444322730567)

PRE-DEPARTURE READING

★

Lonely Planet's *Georgia, Armenia & Azerbaijan* guidebook

★

Bread & Ashes: A Walk Through the Mountains of Georgia by Tony Anderson

★

My Dear Son: The Memoirs of Stalin's Mother by Ekaterine Jughashvili

★

A Man Was Going Down the Road by Otar Chiladze

INTERNET SPEEDS

Typical public wi-fi download speeds hover around the 10 Mbps mark, but faster connections aren't hard to find, though you might struggle at the top end of the spectrum. Pick up a local SIM for reliable 4G connections.

Ways to unwind

Take a sulphur bath – overlook the eggy odour and plunge into the sulphurous waters of the dozen-odd bathhouses in Tbilisi's Abanotubani district, said to heal skin and soothe aching joints.

—

Take in the views from Mtatsminda Park – a funicular train whisks people high above the city for giddying views, forest walks and a collection of endearingly dated amusements, including the country's biggest Ferris wheel.

—

Make for the Caucasus – Kazbegi National Park is just three hours from Tbilisi by *marshrutka*, and opens up the full glory of the Caucasus mountains.

Practicalities

✈ Incheon International Airport, Seoul

LGBT-friendly
Yes

💼 The Republic's isolated neighbour to the north makes overland travel tricky; trains connect almost everywhere inside Korea's borders and ferries run to Japan and mainland China.

📅 March to May and September to November are the best months to enjoy Seoul; temperatures are mild, and spring and autumn bring the brilliant natural colours of blossom and falling leaves. Summers are hot and humid, the polar opposite of Seoul's bitter, icy winters.

$ From US$1000 per month

Seoul, South Korea

If you like your co-working with easy access to grilled ribs, all-night saunas, 24-hour soju (clear liquor) bars and a soundtrack of K-pop, this is the right place. The Republic of Korea's capital is emerging as a thoroughly dynamic place to do business, with a young, entrepreneurial population and the world's fastest internet access. It's everything you'd expect of a futuristic Asian metropolis.

Pros & cons

GREAT FOR:
★ 24-hour working
★ Friendly locals and expats
★ Fantastic food
★ Cutting edge technology
★ Excellent public transport

NOT SO GREAT FOR:
★ Bearable winters and summers
★ Affordable groceries
★ Manageable traffic
★ Cross-cultural understanding
★ Non-speakers of Korean

The fact that Seoul lies off the standard backpacker trail only adds to its appeal as a place to live and work; new arrivals will find a solid support base of resident expats to help with the transition of diving into a new culture. Co-working spaces are everywhere in tech-obsessed Seoul, and the city's dynamic, 24-hour lifestyle makes it easy to work at any time of day or night – handy for connecting with clients in awkward time zones.

English is not spoken everywhere, which can be a help and a hindrance – there are plentiful opportunities here for teachers and translators, but some aspects of day-to-day living are complicated by the language barrier. Korea definitely does things its own way; locals adhere to myriad unspoken social rules, and there's no obvious explanation for the fact that while dining out is cheap, groceries are eye-wateringly expensive.

CO-WORKING SPACES

★ For an in-built sense of community, **Hive Arena** (www.hivearena.com) combines co-living and co-working, in a handy location just south of the Han River in Yeongdeungpo-gu. It's small scale and personal, which many people appreciate in this teeming megacity.

★ Over in Seongdong-gu, **Cow&Dog** (www. cowndog.com) is a co-working space specifically for nomads working on projects with a social impact. It's a popular spot for local entrepreneurs and developers, who rate the calm work environment and ethical approach.

LIVING ARRANGEMENTS

Seoul has plentiful accommodation but prices in the centre are steep. There are lots of nomad-oriented hostels with combined co-living/co-working packages, but many longer-term residents rent apartments or rooms through Airbnb. Gangnam-gu is for high-fliers only, but areas close to the US Army HQ in Yongsan-gu are well set up for nomads; try Itaewon-dong and Haebangchon-dong. Cheap street food includes *kimbap* (rice rolls), *tteokbokki* (rice cakes in spicy sauce), or look for 24-hour joints serving *bibimbap* (stone pot rice) and ramen. Barbecue meals at *gogi-jip* ('meat houses') can also be surprisingly affordable. Get around by subway, bus or taxi.

© ZKRUGER / SHUTTERSTOCK

Previous page: Seoul skyline; Left: Korean street food; Opposite: Bukhansan National Park.

NETWORKING

★ **Seoul Digital Nomads** (www.facebook.com/ seouldigitalentrepreneurs)
★ **Seoul Expats** (www.facebook.com/groups/seoulexpats)
★ **Every Expat in Korea** (www.facebook.com/ groups/2370296695)

PRE-DEPARTURE READING

★

Lonely Planet's *Korea* guidebook and *Pocket Seoul*

★

The Vegetarian by Han Kang

★

Please Look After Mother by Kyung-Sook Shin

★

The New Koreans by Michael Breen

INTERNET SPEEDS

As of 2017, Seoul officially has the fastest public internet access in the world. The city-wide average download speed is 28.6 Mbps, but many co-working spaces offer far faster connections. And with Samsung in town, this is one of the best cities in the world for 5G, with lightning-fast mobile internet if you have a device that is 5G-ready.

Ways to unwind

Dip your toes in Cheong-gye-cheon Stream – locals come to eat packed lunches, read books and dangle their feet in the water of this landscaped artificial stream, formerly the site of a highway.

—

Take a picnic to Gyeongui Line Forest Park – now a long strip of parkland, the former route of the vanished Gyeongui Line has picnic spaces, book stores in mocked-up train carriages and plenty of places to pick up a snack or a craft beer.

—

Temple-hop in Bukhansan National Park – high above the city, this gorgeous landscape of rocky outcrops and forest trails is scattered with Buddhist temples and Joseon-era fortifications.

Practicalities

✈ Ministro Pistarini International, Buenos Aires

LGBT-friendly
Yes

💼 Buses run to all neighbouring countries, and boats zip from Buenos Aires to Montevideo and Colonia in Uruguay.

📅 Buenos Aires has a short, hot summer (December to February), with regular heat spikes and a risk of thunderstorms; the winter (June to August) feels like a European spring. The shoulder seasons bring pleasantly warm (not hot) conditions, but regular rain showers.

$ From US$1100 per month

Buenos Aires, Argentina

Argentina's biggest city vibrates with activity, from the day to the tango-filled night. Many nomads are drawn to Buenos Aires by its Latin flavour, uninhibited nightlife, low living costs and immersive local culture. If you come here to work, and leave without learning Spanish, tango and the importance of a gauchada (good deed), you've missed out on a big part of the fun of living in the city.

Becoming a *porteño* (port city dweller) is only part of the appeal. Buenos Aires has a well-established co-working culture, plenty of local start-ups, and a lively expat community to plug into on arrival. Speaking Spanish will bring dividends for expanding your social network here. BA's local government is also looking to approach entrepreneurs with projects such as IncuBAte, which offers support and subsidies for startups that have a tangible benefit to the city.

However, nomads have some administrative hoops to leap through during extended stays in Buenos Aires. Most travellers are granted visa-free entry to Argentina for 90 days on arrival; if you want to stay longer, you'll have to get used to nipping over to neighbouring countries for a new entry stamp, or applying for a *prórroga* (visa extension). To avoid the hassle, many nomads simply overstay and pay a moderate fine at the airport on departure.

Pros & cons

GREAT FOR:
★ Culture
★ Nightlife
★ Low cost of living
★ Expat lifestyle
★ Cheap public transport

NOT SO GREAT FOR:
★ Traffic noise
★ Urban sprawl
★ Petty crime
★ Crowds
★ Currency fluctuations

CO-WORKING SPACES

★ For co-working and co-living in one space, NomadHub (www.nomadh.co) in Retiro offers smart rooms and workspaces, fast wi-fi and a strong community spirit in a handy location just southeast of Palermo. It's a good first stop before setting up on your own, once you're familiar with the city.

★ If your remote working model depends on good coffee, march your laptop along to Café Flor (www.cafeflor.com.ar), where co-workers pay by the hour for fast internet access, with as much coffee as you can drink thrown into the package.

LIVING ARRANGEMENTS

Buenos Aires has a scattering of co-living spaces that are great for new arrivals, but longer term residents tend to look for rooms to rent. There's a culture of over-charging, so for rooms at the same prices locals pay, ask around on expat forums and Facebook groups. Fresh from the airport, many travellers go overboard on red meat and wine at inexpensive local parrillas (grill-houses), but healthier food isn't hard to find. For cheap eats, seek out mom-and-pop snack-stops serving empanadas (pasties) and morcipán and choripán sausage sandwiches. All parts of the city can be reached cheaply via the subway or local buses.

© ELXENEIZE / SHUTTERSTOCK

Previous page: Buenos Aires skyline; Left: La Boca district; Opposite: Floralis Genérica sculpture, Plaza Naciones Unidas.

NETWORKING

★ Buenos Aires Expats Community (www.baexpats.org)
★ Buenos Aires Expat Hub (www.facebook.com/groups/BuenosAiresExpatHub)

PRE-DEPARTURE READING

★
Lonely Planet's *Argentina* and *Buenos Aires* guidebooks
★
The Tango Singer by Tomás Eloy Martínez
★
La Autopista del Sur y Otros Cuentos by Julio Cortázar
★
My Fathers' Ghost Is Climbing in the Rain by Patricio Pron

INTERNET SPEEDS

Download speeds of 16 Mbps are easy to find, and co-working spaces offer much faster connections. Most cafes have free wi-fi and the government provides free public connections in many parks, plazas and public spaces. Mobile 4G connections are easy to find, but download speeds can be lower than expected.

Ways to unwind

Learn to tango – tourist-oriented shows abound, but for the real deal, visit a local milonga if you like to join locals dancing purely for the love of dance. Try Milonga Parakultural at Salón Canning in Palermo.

—

Mingle with the dead at Recoleta Cemetery - the city's most famous cemetery is a tangled maze of pathways, lined with the grand mausoleums of wealthy Porteños, including the revered tomb of Eva Perón.

—

Explore the Paraná Delta – when the city gets too much, jump on a train to Tigre, and rent a motorboat or kayak to roam around the interconnected canals and waterways, or browse the waterfront craft market.

© PHILIP LEE HARVEY/LONELY PLANET

Practicalities

✈ Chiang Mai International Airport, Chiang Mai

LGBT-friendly
Yes

🧳 Trains and buses run to cities across Thailand, with easy border crossings to Laos, Myanmar, Cambodia and Malaysia.

📅 The dry season (November–March) sees clear skies and manageable daytime temperatures, but the mercury rises to uncomfortable levels from April to June. The monsoon (July–October) brings torrential rains that flood roads and drive residents indoors.

$ From US$1000 per month

Chiang Mai, Thailand

Thailand's second city has long been a hangout for globetrotting techies, thanks to a perfect combination of cheap accommodation, fast wi-fi and spectacular food at penny prices. Not many other hubs are this well set up for nomads, with everything you could need downtown, and easy escapes to jungle-covered mountains, waterfalls, hot springs and ancient monasteries beyond the city limits.

Co-working spaces abound and internet access can be blindingly fast, accommodation is cheap, clean and comfortable, and the city fizzes with energy after dark, so what's not to like? Well, the levels of tourism for one thing. With the surge in cheap flights to other parts of Asia, the city is mobbed by travellers pretty much every day of the year. If you like to immerse yourself in local culture, Chiang Mai may not be the place.

On the other hand, the quality of life is hard to deny. You could eat a different dish every day for a year in Chiang Mai and still be just scratching the surface. Be aware though that Thailand's visa system is inconvenient for nomads – visitors get 30-days on arrival (or 60 days with a pre-arranged visa), and only one 30-day extension is permitted, so you'll have to get used to making the visa run to neighbouring countries to stay more than a few months.

Pros & cons

GREAT FOR:
★ Cheap food and accommodation
★ Nightlife
★ Fast internet
★ Easy escapes to the countryside
★ Good transport links

NOT SO GREAT FOR:
★ Crowds
★ Overtourism
★ Avoiding tropical heat
★ Traffic (outside the old town)
★ Smog

© MATT MUNRO / LONELY PLANET

CO-WORKING SPACES

★ With three city campuses – Nimman, Pratu Tha Phae and Wiang Kaew – **Punspace** (www. punspace.com) is great for nomads who want a bit of working-space variety. As well as fast access and cool air-con, it has meeting rooms and booths for phone calls. You can pay by the day or sign up for a long-term membership.

★ On top of the swish Maya mall in the north of the city, **C.A.M.P. Ais** (www.ais.co.th/campais/en) has the advantage of being sponsored by Thailand's biggest mobile phone company, meaning download speeds of up to 300 Mbps. It's open 24-hours for members, and the mall is jammed with restaurants and cafes if you need a change of scenery.

© DAVID SALA / 500PX

LIVING ARRANGEMENTS

Hotels and hostels are so cheap that many nomads are happy to keep living the backpacker life, but if you crave your own space, serviced apartments and rooms for rent are easy to find. Many nomads base themselves in the walled old town for the abundance of places to eat, drink and party, but rates are lower in the less salubrious Chang Khlan area, or the student quarter of Chang Phueak. For the best street food, hit the Talat Pratu Chang Pheuak and Talat Pratu Chiang Mai evening markets, or browse the stalls at the Saturday and Sunday Walking Street markets. Get around by chartered túk-túk or *rót daang* (chartered truck).

Previous page: Songkran sand pagodas in Chiang Mai; Left: Thai street food; Opposite: Wat Chedi Luang.

PRE-DEPARTURE READING

★

Lonely Planet's *Thailand* guidebook

★

Anna and the King of Siam by Margaret Landon

★

Sightseeing by Rattawut Lapcharoensap

★

Fieldwork by Mischa Berlinski

NETWORKING

★ **Chiang Mai Digital Nomads** (www.facebook.com/groups/cmnomads)

✱ **Digital Nomad Coffee Club** – Chiang Mai (www.facebook.com/groups/nomadcoffee)

✱ **Welcome Chiang Mai Nomads!** (www.facebook.com/groups/WelcomeChiangMaiNomads)

INTERNET SPEEDS

Chiang Mai is extremely well connected, and almost everywhere to stay and eat offers free wi-fi. Download speeds of 26 Mbps are common, and co-working spaces offer much faster wired optical cable connections of 300 Mbps or more. Pick up a local SIM for fast 4G access without the crippling costs of data roaming on your home phone.

© GABOR KOVACS PHOTOGRAPHY / SHUTTERSTOCK

Ways to unwind

Climb above the city at Wat Phra That Doi Suthep – the motorcycle or mountain-bike ride to Chiang Mai's most famous stupa is the city's favourite way to unwind, or you can trek up from the Chiang Mai University campus.

—

Swim in waterfalls and hot springs – escape the tourist crowds by zipping out to jungle cascades and natural hot springs on a rented motorcycle or a chartered *rót daang*.

—

Choose your own jungle escape – the forested peaks surrounding Chiang Mai are dotted with rural resorts that offer a welcome respite from the city heat. Chiang Dao and Doi Inthanon National Park are great spots for an overnight retreat.

Practicalities

✈ Budapest Ferenc Liszt International Airport, Budapest

LGBT-friendly
Yes

💼 Trains and buses connect Budapest to cities across Europe.

📅 Budapest has a classic continental climate, with a hot summer (with occasional heavy rainfall) and, thanks to frigid air masses from Russia, a bitterly cold winter from December to February. The most pleasant months are April to May and September to October.

$ From US$1200 per month

Budapest, Hungary

Looking for the grandeur of Paris or Rome without the high prices? Welcome to Budapest, serving up three historic cities – Buda, Óbuda and Pest – for the price of one. Modest living costs and light-speed internet place Budapest high on the wish list for digital nomads who rate atmosphere as much as amenities; it's also the perfect gateway for exploring Eastern Europe and the Balkans.

Though the tourist crowds deter some, the Hungarian capital is great for cheap digs and cheap eats, and the cheapest beers in Europe make it easy to wind down at the end of a work day. Co-working spaces and cafes with wi-fi are easy to find, and the continental climate is easier to live with than the year-round heat of Bali or Thailand, though many flee to warmer climes in winter.

As for cons, the start-up scene is still small, so the sense of community among remote workers and entrepreneurs is less developed than in more established remote working hubs. Hook up with other nomads in the city's co-working spaces and on nomad Facebook groups. Hungary is in the Schengen Area so most nationalities get a visa-free 90-day stay on arrival that also allows free travel to surrounding countries; to stay longer, you'll need to apply for residence or for a long-stay visa before you travel.

Pros & cons

GREAT FOR:
★ Low cost of living
★ Cheap eats
★ Pocket-friendly nightlife
★ Good public transport
★ Easy access to other European hubs

NOT SO GREAT FOR:
★ Infrastructure
★ Tourist crowds
★ Bearable winters
★ Begging and homelessness
★ Understanding the local language

CO-WORKING SPACES

★ There's a strong community vibe at **Kaptar** (www.kaptarbudapest.hu/en) on the fringes of Inner City in Pest, with regular meetups and networking events. It's a great place to be based for exploring the city on lunch breaks, and there's an on-site coffee shop keeping nomads in refreshments through the day.

★ With a handy central location on the east bank, near the south end of Margaret Island, **Kubik Coworking** (www.kubikcoworking.hu/en) has well-equipped shared spaces, private offices and meeting rooms, and it offers day passes as well as membership packages.

LIVING ARRANGEMENTS

Prices are high in the centre, so most nomads eat and sleep in the suburbs. District XI in Buda, and Districts IX, VI and VII in Pest are popular bases, but rents are often hiked for non-Hungarians. Many nomads start off in a short-term Airbnb before tracking down rented rooms or apartments by speaking to co-workers. Alberlet (www.alberlet.hu/en) and Ingatlan (www.ingatlan.com) have lots of listings, and going through a local estate agent can help break down language barriers. Save money by eating at local restaurants with daily specials, and snacking on street food *langos* (fried bread topped with sour cream and cheese). Forego expensive taxis for the metro, bus or tram.

© 2020. KAPTAR. BUDAPEST / PH. ATTILA OZSE - OZSEATTILA.COM

Previous page: Budapest Parliament; Left: Co-working at Kaptar; Opposite: Liberty Bridge.

NETWORKING

★ Digital Nomads Budapest
(www.facebook.com/groups/648464231947085).
★ Digital Nomad Hungary
(www.facebook.com/digitalnomadhungary)
★ Hungary EXPATS
(www.facebook.com/groups/hungary.expats)

PRE-DEPARTURE READING

★

Lonely Planet's *Budapest & Hungary* and *Pocket Budapest* guidebook

★

Fatelessness
by Imre Kertész

★

The Invisible Bridge
by Julie Orringer

★

Enemies of the People
by Kati Marton

INTERNET SPEEDS

Download speeds of 27 Mbps or higher are easy to find, and wi-fi is widespread in city cafes, public parks and shopping centres. The city also claims to have the world's third-fastest 4G network.

Ways to unwind

Have a Hungarian bath – the Gellért is the city's most famous bathhouse, but Budapest is dotted with smaller spas where you can enjoy thermal springs with less company. Most baths are mixed, but more traditional Turkish-style baths are often men-only.

—

Jog around Margaret Island – a soft running track skirts the edge of Margaret Island, passing parkland, fountains and flower gardens, plus the open-air waterslides and splash pools of the Palatinus Baths.

—

Haggle for bargains in the Ecseri Flea Market – you'll find genuine Soviet-era heirlooms among the general junk at this sprawling bazaar southeast of Pest.

© LINGXIAO XIE / GETTY IMAGES

Practicalities

✈ Gran Canaria Airport, Los Moriscos

LGBT-friendly
Yes

🧳 Ferries run to Las Palmas from Cadiz and Huelva on the Spanish mainland.

📅 Gran Canaria's southerly latitude means warm temperatures year-round, tempered by ocean breezes. Most rain falls between October and February, and locals head to the west coast in February and March, when *calima* dust storms can blow in from North Africa.

$ From €1100 per month

Las Palmas de Gran Canaria, Spain

A little bit of Europe tacked onto the edge of North Africa, Gran Canaria can thank its year-round warm weather for its status as one of the world's top remote working destinations. Plentiful co-working spaces, fast net access and a big pool of fellow nomads all add to the attraction. Many nomads work the summer in other parts of Europe and come to Gran Canaria for the balmy winter.

As well as the climate, expats and visiting remote workers rave about the human scale of Las Palmas. The Canary Islands' eclectic capital is large enough to have everything you need, but still small enough to explore on foot or by bike. And it offers lots of possibilities for downtime: head to the beach, go surfing, windsurfing or scuba-diving, or tackle the trails that crisscross the island's interior on foot or by mountain bike.

While it's easy to stay active, living cheaply here is more of a challenge. Rents, while lower than on the mainland, can still eat into your budget, and cheap eats are also hard to track down. Being treated like a tourist, even if you're here all year round, can also wear a bit thin. Bear in mind, too, that moving on from Gran Canaria by air can be costly; instead, consider one of the inexpensive ferries that run to Cádiz and Huelva on the Spanish mainland.

Pros & cons

GREAT FOR:
- ★ Perfect weather
- ★ Staying active
- ★ Beachlife
- ★ Tax-free drinking
- ★ Community

NOT SO GREAT FOR:
- ★ Nomads on a budget
- ★ Non-Spanish speakers
- ★ Sandstorms
- ★ Affordable overseas travel
- ★ Tourist crowds

CO-WORKING SPACES

★ Leading the way in Las Palmas, **CoworkingC** (www.coworkingc.com) is just steps from the beach, but its workspaces are calm and conducive to productivity. Members can download at speeds of 300 Mbps or more day and night, and even day passes include unlimited coffee.

★ **The House** (www.the-house.eu) falls somewhere between co-working space and home, with two kitchens, twin roof decks, free coffee and breakfast, and Spanish lessons to help remote workers integrate into the local co-working community.

LIVING ARRANGEMENTS

Finding a room or apartment to rent in Gran Canaria is easy via Airbnb, international villa-rental sites and local agents, and wi-fi is often included in the price. Affordability increases the further you get from the coast, and negotiating a fair rate gets easier if you speak a little Spanish. Budget eats are harder to find than on the mainland – look out for cheap *menu del dia* (set lunch menus) at local Spanish restaurants. Taxis are expensive; stick to local buses and walk or rent a bicycle.

© CRIBEN / SHUTTERSTOCK

Previous page: Las Canteras beach; Left: Pozo Izquierdo windsurfing; Opposite: Canary Islands hike.

NETWORKING

★ Gran Canaria Digital Nomad (www.facebook.com/groups/201877786658754)
★ Las Palmas Info (www.facebook.com/groups/1648535165253439)
★ Gran Canaria Expat Community (www.facebook.com/groups/MovingToGranCanaria)

PRE-DEPARTURE READING

★

Lonely Planet's *Canary Islands* guidebook

★

Lanzarote by Michel Houellebecq

★

The Drago Tree by Isobel Blackthorn

★

More Ketchup than Salsa by Joe Cawley

INTERNET SPEEDS

Wi-fi and hard-wired connections are fast in co-working spaces – 300 Mbps upwards – but slower in Las Palmas cafes, and positively sluggish (5 Mbps or less) once you leave the centre of the city. Local SIM cards with 4G access are widely available.

Ways to unwind

Hit the beach – busy Las Canteras runs for 3.5km along the east side of Las Palmas and is crowded with sunseekers in season; there are calmer strips of sand to the north at El Confital or south at San Cristobal.

—

Windsurf the east coast – windsurfers flock to the windblown shoreline at Pozo Izquierdo and Salinas for warm, fast winds in summer; try Bahia de Formas for flat, freestyle-friendly water.

—

Hike to Roque Nublo – this thumb-like nub of volcanic rock is reached via a scenic 5km hike over forest-covered outcrops, with epic views over the island. Numerous other routes cross the island.

© CANADASTOCK / SHUTTERSTOCK

Practicalities

✈ Lennart Meri Tallinn Airport, Tallinn

LGBT-friendly
Yes

💼 Buses connect to Tallinn from across Europe, while trains run to local destinations and to Moscow and St Petersburg. Fast, frequent ferries run to Helsinki and Stockholm.

📅 Warm days and sporadic showers mark Tallinn's short summer from June to August. Spring and autumn are cooler but still pleasant enough for cafe working. The long, bitter winter is the sting – snow arrives in November and can linger till April.

$ From €1000 per month

Tallinn, Estonia

Travellers love Estonia's tiny cobblestoned capital for its moderate costs, Unesco-listed old town and stepping-stone position between Eastern Europe, the Nordic states and Russia. For digital nomads, it's the business-friendly attitude and start-up culture that appeals. Tallinn is one of Europe's top three cities for start-ups per capita, beating long-established Eurozone tech hubs.

To tempt overseas talent, Estonia's e-Residency scheme (www.e-resident.gov.ee) allows online businesses to set up here remotely; a start-up visa (www.startupestonia.ee) gives special support to foreign entrepreneurs who set up within the country. This will soon be joined by a new visa aimed at digital nomads, allowing them to live and work in Estonia for up to a year, including for local companies. And EU citizens, of course, can set up here with few restrictions.

While central Tallinn can get busy with both cruise ship crowds and raucous stag party and hen night groups at weekends, the city has nonetheless managed to hold onto its enigmatic identity, and the hordes evaporate as the long, cold winter approaches. Plentiful co-working spaces will keep you warm and connected, even when snow gathers outside, and the sense of community among remote workers is tangible year-round.

Pros & cons

GREAT FOR:
★ Start-ups
★ Nomad-friendly visa policies
★ Support from local government
★ Sense of community
★ Low cost of living

NOT SO GREAT FOR:
★ Cruise ship crowds
★ Bearable winters
★ Affordable rents
★ Budget shopping
★ Free public transport (its restricted to residents)

CO-WORKING SPACES

★ With a handy Telliskivi location **Lift 99** (www.lift99.co) has a strong community vibe and lots of start-up-themed meets and seminars. Members can access its fast net, workstations, meeting spaces, and chill-out areas (including a ping-pong table and library) at all hours.

★ Just south of the centre in Kristiine, **Spring Hub** (www.springhub.org) is large and calm, with a quiet atmosphere that encourages productivity. There are straight-up work spaces, beanbag areas and an open-plan kitchen where you can chat to other freelancers.

LIVING ARRANGEMENTS

Many nomads start off in hostels (several specifically target remote workers) or rooms arranged through Airbnb, before moving on to rented rooms or apartments. Accommodation in the Old Town is limited and expensive, but the nearby neighbourhoods of Kalamaja, Telliskivi and Noblessner have a Bohemian vibe and lower rents for rooms and apartments. Save money by eating out away from the centre; look for cheap daily specials on chalkboards and handwritten menus. Public transport in Tallinn – by bus, trolleybus and tram – is free for city residents, inexpensive for visitors, or hail a cab via Bolt (www.bolt.eu/en-gb).

© 2020. SPRING HUB, TALLINN

Previous page: Winter in Tallinn; Left: Springhub co-working space; Opposite: Cafe culture, central Tallinn.

PRE-DEPARTURE READING

★

Lonely Planet's *Estonia, Latvia & Lithuania* guidebook

★

Treading Air by Jaan Kross

★

Truth and Justice: Andres and Pearu by Anton H Tammsaare

★

Purge by Sofi Oksanen

NETWORKING

★ Digital Nomads Tallinn (www.facebook.com/Digital-Nomads-Tallinn-448230495534489)
★ Expats in Tallinn, Estonia (www.facebook.com/groups/1395659303995885)
★ Tallinn Expats (www.facebook.com/groups/tallinnexpats)

INTERNET SPEEDS

Free wi-fi is found almost everywhere, and web users in Tallinn can expect download speeds of 20 Mbps or higher, and much faster connections in co-working spaces. Estonian mobile network Elisa offers 100% 4G coverage in the city.

Ways to unwind

Climb the Teletorn – the best views of Tallinn are from the top of this television tower, set in an area of pine-forest northeast of the centre; on a clear day, you can see as far as Finland on the far side of the Gulf.

—

Head to the beach in Pirita – a short bus ride from downtown, this seaside suburb has the city's largest and loveliest beach, backed by pines and with such handy amenities as changing cabins and a beach bar in summer.

—

Go wild in Lahemaa National Park – just 70km east of Tallinn, Lahemaa's forests, lakes, bogland, rocky cliffs and beaches harbour moose, wild boar, brown bears and lynxes.

Practicalities

✈ Cancún International Airport, Cancún

LGBT-friendly
Yes

🧳 Buses run to Playa del Carmen from across Mexico, with easy transfers across the border to the US, Belize, Guatemala and beyond.

📅 December to April brings perfect weather (and tourists) to the Riviera Maya. Tourist crowds lessen from May to August, but high temperatures and humidity can be uncomfortable. September to November see peak rainfall and possible tropical storms.

$ From US$1000 per month

Playa Del Carmen, Mexico

Plenty of digital nomads head to Mexico to take advantage of the tropical vibe and to avoid the red tape involved with remote working in the USA. The Yucatán peninsula has always been the top chill-out spot, and Playa del Carmen is the favourite digital nomad hangout, with a lively cafe and co-working culture, fast connections, and easy access to beaches, reefs, ruins and cenotes (sinkholes).

In atmosphere and spirit, Playa del Carmen leans more toward backpacker Tulum than package-tour Cancún. Nonetheless, this pretty beach town is firmly angled toward outsiders, so nomads looking for an authentic Mexican experience may be a little disappointed. On the other hand, there's a strong sense of community here among remote workers, and plenty of other nomads to share the experience with.

Travellers from most countries can stay for 180 days without a visa, but border officials generally stamp either 30, 60 or 90 days on the Forma Migratoria Multiple (FMM) you are granted on arrival. If you plan to stay longer, either explain to the officials when you arrive (you may need to show an onward ticket and proof of funds to support yourself), extend with the local immigration office, or cross the border to a neighbouring state and re-enter with a new FMM.

Pros & cons

GREAT FOR:
★ Cost of living
★ US-friendly time zone
★ Strong sense of community
★ Tropical weather
★ Adventure activities in non-work time

NOT SO GREAT FOR:
★ Affordable food
★ Avoiding crowds in season
★ Diverse culture
★ Variety

★ Central, smart and fast, **Nest Coworking** (www. coworkingnest.com.mx/en) has a sustainable ethos, a strong community spirit, and a regular program of events, networking sessions and socials. There's coffee, a kitchen, and hammocks to chill on (this is Mexico, after all).

★ If you don't mind heading inland from the beach, **Work Zone Coworking** (www.oficinasplaya.com) offers a quiet work environment, lower prices and a chance to connect with the local remote-working community. There's a simple cafe, and a wealth of eating options nearby.

Many start with Airbnb accommodation but there are plenty of rooms and apartments for rent for longer-term stays. There are loads of local letting agents, or try asking around on expat-oriented Facebook groups, or at co-working spaces. For cheap eats, avoid the touristy spots around La Quinta Avenida and dine in local restaurants, or graze on street food: tacos, burritos and tortas. The city bus and *colectivo* (shared van) network is limited, so get used to walking, riding a bike or taking a taxi.

Previous page: Playa del Carmen; Left: Cenote paddleboarding; Opposite: Diving at Chac-Mool cenote.

© STOCKCAM / GETTY IMAGES

NETWORKING

★ Digital Nomads Playa Del Carmen Cancun Tulum (www. facebook.com/groups/1608835499405356)

★ Expats in Playa del Carmen (www.facebook.com/ groups/1433838026828456)

★ Real Estate for Expats in Playa del Carmen (www.facebook. com/groups/589843537856986)

PRE-DEPARTURE READING

★

Lonely Planet's *Mexico and Cancún, Cozumel & the Yucatán* guidebook

★

Incidents of Travel in Yucatán by John L Stephens

★

The Falling Woman by Pat Murphy

★

Digging in Yucatán by Ann Axtell Morris

INTERNET SPEEDS

Wi-fi is everywhere in Playa del Carmen and, while not lightspeed, download speeds of 10 Mbps are common; and many co-working spaces offer speeds of ten times that. AT&T/Unefon offers patchy 4G coverage in the centre.

© LUIS JAVIER SANDOVAL / GETTY IMAGES

Ways to unwind

Snorkel or dive off Cozumel – a 40-minute ferry ride from Playa del Carmen will drop you in one of the Caribbean's diving playgrounds; or you can snorkel straight off the rocks on the west coast.

—

Rent a cabaña at Tulum – with its beachhuts, crystal waters, Mayan ruins and rainforest reserves, laid-back Tulum serves up the best of the Mayan peninsula; it's popular, but arrive at the ruins of Tulum or Cobá at opening time and you'll still feel like a jungle explorer.

—

Swim in a sinkhole – dive into pools of impossible blue amid the tropical forest; Cenote Chaak Tun is within the Playa del Carmen city limits.

Alternative digital nomad destinations

Having had their time in the sun, early nomad hubs such as Barcelona and Prague are being replaced by new hotspots, often at the exciting fringes of the travel map. Free spirits who crave cultural immersion – and can get by with less support from fellow nomads – have the whole world to choose from. Here are some interesting spots for the adventurous.

© CHUYU / ISTOCK / GETTY IMAGES

3 XI'AN, CHINA

China might not be an obvious choice as a base for digital nomads, but second-tier cities such as Xi'an offer a fascinating work environment, amazing food, low living costs and a chance to plug into one of the world's most dynamic economies. However, learning Mandarin is a prerequisite for getting the best out of the city.

1 TIRANA, ALBANIA

It wasn't that long ago that even visiting Albania as a tourist was for adventurers only, but since opening up to the world, the Albania capital has a lot to tempt digital nomads: inexpensive food and rooms, hospitable citizens and an astonishing density of cafes with cheap coffee and free wi-fi. Just be ready for quieter-than-average nightlife and a limited selection of co-working spaces.

2 BELGRADE, SERBIA

People often overlook the Serbian capital because of its troubled history, but the cost of living is low, the internet is reliable, and there's plenty of co-working space in and around the historic centre. It's a good choice for people looking for a quiet space to hunker down and build a business, with all the Balkan states on the doorstep for weekend exploration.

4 LVIV, UKRAINE

Lviv is emerging as a dynamic place to do business. Ukraine's least Soviet city has a fabulous coffeehouse scene, a rich culture and plenty of co-working spaces with speedy internet. Its compact and architecturally lovely centre will appeal to many remote workers, especially with its low cost of living and great access to Kraków, Poland and the rest of Europe.

5 BOCAS DEL TORO, PANAMA

A string of idyllic Caribbean islands might not sound like an obvious place to put in a hard day's work, but the Bocas del Toro Archipelago has a small but growing network of co-working spaces and an expanding nomad community. Come for the beach life, stay for the wi-fi seems to be the motto; break up your work time with scuba diving, national park trips and buzzing nightlife.

© DAMSEA / SHUTTERSTOCK

© GRISHA BRIJEV / SHUTTERSTOCK

7 TARIFA, SPAIN

With soaring living costs, Barcelona has dropped off the must-do list for many digital nomads, but laid-back Tarifa, on the coast of Andalusia near Cádiz, has emerged as a burgeoning hub for travellers who like a little kitesurfing with their remote working. Infrastructure is modest but expanding, with a handful of co-working hostels and dedicated workspaces, as well as cafes with free wi-fi.

9 TAGHAZOUT, MOROCCO

Morocco has a long history of unconventional expats, and digital nomads are just the latest crew to set up shop on the North African coast. With a expanding start-up scene, speedy internet and great actual surfing as well as web-surfing, Taghazout is popular with nomads at the bohemian end of the spectrum – great for those who rate time off as highly as work time.

© DIANA JARVIS

6 BISHKEK, KYRGYZSTAN

Cheap, spacious accommodation, solid tech infrastructure, and easy visa runs to Kazakhstan are big drawcards for the Kyrgyz capital. As with many cities in former Soviet states, Bishkek lies off the mainstream travel map, but the mountains are an adventurous playground for the times when you aren't typing out code in co-working spaces.

8 SOFIA, BULGARIA

For nomads, there's a lot to like about Sofia: pocket-friendly living, fast internet, rich history, abundant co-working spaces, and easy travel to Greece, Turkey, Romania and the Balkans. Bulgaria's delayed entry to the Schengen zone also makes this an easy place for non-Europeans to travel and work. The nomad scene is small – if you crave a big network, this might not be the place for you.

10 QUITO, ECUADOR

Joining the growing ranks of South American cities with a nomad buzz, Quito offers a different experience. The Ecuadorian capital is the gateway to the Andes, promising plenty of hardcore adventures for the days away from its cafes and co-working spaces. Visas are another plus: most nationalities get free entry for 90 days on arrival, and the option to extend for a further 90.

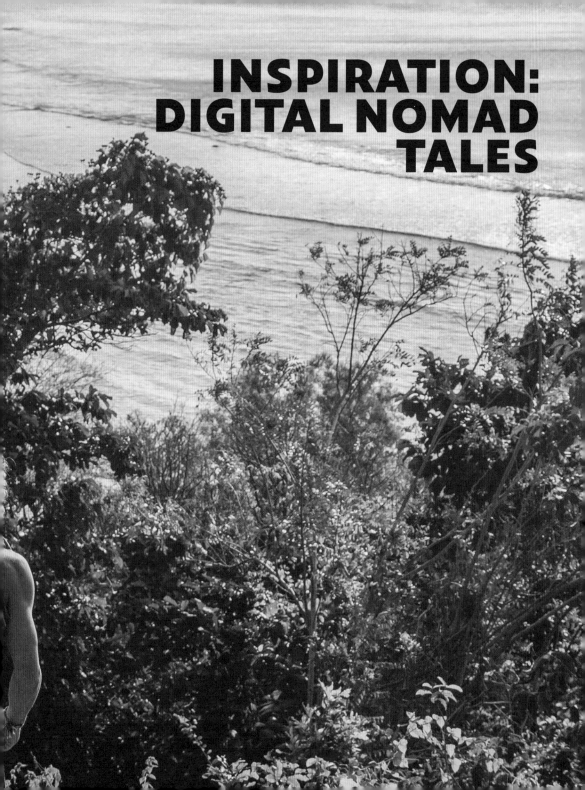

INSPIRATION:
DIGITAL NOMAD
TALES

Matthew Kepnes

Matt Kepnes, writer and founder of
www.nomadicmatt.com

WHAT WERE YOU DOING BEFORE YOU BECAME A DIGITAL NOMAD?

Before I started travelling, I was doing the same thing as most Americans: working 9 to 5. I had finished college and worked as a hospital administrator in Boston, the town where I grew up. On a vacation to Thailand in 2005 I met some backpackers, and that encounter created a paradigm shift that led me to quit my job and travel the world. As soon as I got home I saved up all my money, worked a ton of overtime, and then quit my job to travel.

WHAT MADE YOU DECIDE TO START A TRAVEL BLOG?

My original idea was to use my blog as a springboard to find paid writing gigs. In the back of my mind I had the idea that I could write for Lonely Planet, travelling the world like some kind of Bill Bryson–Anthony Bourdain mix. I definitely didn't have any idea the blog would be a success when I first started.

When I started, the tech aspect of things had me pulling out my hair more times than I can count. Learning WordPress, SEO, how to write, and how to promote my writing was an uphill battle. But as my traffic started to grow, I started to spend more time on my writing and started to treat my website like the potential business that it could be. The more I did it, the more I liked it, the better I got, and the more I wanted to keep doing it.

WHAT WOULD YOU SAY WERE THE BIGGEST CHALLENGES YOU FACED?

I think self-doubt is something most entrepreneurs and self-employed people deal with. Do I have the skills? Can this actually work? And am I stupid for quitting my safe job and taking this risk? Those questions are always floating around the back of your mind and can definitely take their toll if left unchecked. Worry and anxiety are constant challenges but I do my best to always have a solution in my mind to keep them at bay.

DO YOU EVER FEEL LONELY ON THE ROAD?

Working online is pretty far removed from what you see on social media. More often than not, you're hunched over your laptop at a cafe (or airport or hostel or train station or coworking space) typing away the hours. As an introvert, I don't necessarily mind the isolation. But I also know it can take its toll if I don't actively work to engage myself.

It's far too easy to spend day after day in front of your laptop. To avoid this, I'm always looking for local events or meet-ups. There are tons of apps and online platforms to help with this, so anytime I need company I just reach out and see what I can find, and I use these events as a springboard to engage with the wider community.

WHAT ADVICE WOULD YOU GIVE SOMEONE THINKING OF DOING THE SAME THING?

All too often we read about people who just quit their job and jumped into the world of remote work. That's a terrible idea. Always look before you leap! That means having a game plan in place. That means having the skills to get you started. That means having enough savings in your bank account to last. Plan. Prepare. And then dive in.

Jazzie Mas

Jazzie Mas, wellness consultant, online teacher and director of www.blackdigitalnomad.com

WHAT INSPIRED YOU TO BECOME A DIGITAL NOMAD?

Before venturing off to travel the world I was a brand ambassador and health and wellness consultant. I had a small business making organic skincare products and sold them at the local farmers market, but I was still feeling unfulfilled and wanted to live life fully, and the racial divide in America began to feel overwhelming and I wanted out.

My husband and I decided to take six months off to live on the beach in Mexico, and three months in we decided this was how we wanted to live full-time, and we needed to figure out how to make this life work.

HOW DID YOU GO ABOUT FINDING WORK?

While living in Mexico we met other people who were working remotely and started looking into some of the things they were doing for income. In the beginning, we lived off our savings while building our businesses. I continued to do my health coaching, then I started teaching English online and we figured out new ways to turn our passion into profits.

My top tips? Be consistent. Be bold! Starting a business is now easier than ever and because of that, there's even more competition so you have to stand out or get lost in the crowd. Trends are changing often so stay up to date in your field. And there is nothing like in-person connections – go out and network!

WHAT MADE YOU START THE SITE BLACKDIGITALNOMAD?

When I started looking into becoming a digital nomad I did not see anyone who looked like me. Representation matters, and I wanted other people of colour to know that this lifestyle is attainable for us as well. I also wanted a safe space for people of colour to share our experiences without being silenced or told what to do by our white counterparts. My biggest challenge has been getting brands to pay me as much as my white counterparts, especially galling considering how many trends are started by black people. Another challenge is making sure I'm travelling to places that are safe for people of colour.

WHAT HAVE BEEN THE BEST AND WORST (OR RATHER, MOST DIFFICULT) PLACES YOU HAVE BEEN BASED?

I have loved every place we have lived so far: Playa del Carmen, Bali, Chiang Mai, Da Nang Vietnam. The internet in Ubud sucked – and as a digital nomad, the internet is our lifeline – but living around the world has shown me how adaptable I can be.

HAVE YOU FOUND IT EASY TO MAKE A LIVING AS A DIGITAL NOMAD?

It's fairly easy to make money online but building a consistent income for my business hasn't been as easy – it took a lot more work than just logging in and teaching English. Also, with everyone wanting to work remotely the competition is tough.

WHAT ADVICE WOULD YOU GIVE SOMEONE THINKING OF DOING THE SAME THING?

Try it! This lifestyle comes in all different forms so find what works for you. It's definitely possible but it's also not as easy as Instagram makes it look, so don't fall for the hype.

Daniel Clarke

Daniel Clarke, photographer, web designer and blogger at www.danflyingsolo.com

WHAT INSPIRED YOU TO BECOME A DIGITAL NOMAD?

When I got on my one-way flight out of London, I had no idea this was the direction I was heading. I'd just left my job as a restaurant manager, not because I hated it, but because I needed a change. The plan was to travel and work out what was next, and it was in those first months travelling through Southeast Asia and Australia that I realised photography was something I wanted to chase. I also realised anywhere could be an office.

DID YOU HAVE ANY APPREHENSIONS ABOUT STARTING THE NOMAD LIFE?

I skipped all the usual emotions in the lead up to leaving, specifically thoughts about whether becoming a nomad would work and whether I would make enough money. Instead, I went through these emotions later as I began my digital nomad journey, and they were intense; the constant fear of running out of cash was the biggest worry.

A big part of whether you succeed is how far you are happy to push yourself at the start, especially when it's also a new career. There were some pretty miserable lows – from days just eating the same loaf of bread to getting on a flight to a new country not knowing if I'd have been paid an outstanding invoice so I could actually afford the hotel I'd booked.

WHAT HAVE BEEN THE MAIN CHALLENGES?

It has been a rollercoaster at times, and a little more wiggle room in the bank before leaving would have been convenient. I do think I'd over-romanticised the digital nomad life, perhaps because it hadn't really been my intention to become a nomad when I left home. When travelling, I would always see people sitting in cafes, having Skype meetings and seemingly working half days. What I didn't realise was behind all those chilled-looking moments is a constant hunt for good wi-fi and strange working hours.

DO YOU EVER GET LONELY ON THE ROAD?

Being nomadic can sometimes be a bit lonely, so establishing a group of friends when you arrive is helpful. Settling into one place for a little while and getting some 'home comforts' is the best way to avoid nomad burnout and loneliness.

WHAT HAVE BEEN THE BEST AND WORST (OR RATHER, MOST DIFFICULT) PLACES YOU HAVE BEEN BASED?

Bali was the most comfortable spot… there were plenty of co-working venues and a constant stream of visitors. I could join in with the local nomad community a lot more easily. Australia and New Zealand were two of the hardest, as everything was more expensive, and I found more of a permanent co-working crowd than a digital nomad environment.

WHAT ADVICE WOULD YOU GIVE SOMEONE THINKING OF DOING THE SAME THING?

It's always a resounding 'yes' from me when people ask if they should take the digital nomad leap, but having (extra) cash in the bank is undoubtedly the biggest tip I could give anyone. Also, remember to network and build your own nomadic community too.

Doug Murray

Doug Murray, content creator and marketing professional at www.dougmurrayproductions.com

WHAT INSPIRED YOU TO BECOME A DIGITAL NOMAD?

I was employed full-time in the Canadian television industry, working in many different areas over the years – operations, news and marketing , all skills that would be useful in the future – but as I travelled more, I found it difficult to keep my trips confined to just a few weeks a year. I decided that it was better for me to leave full-time work and freelance.

HOW DID YOU FIND WORK?

Having different skills is one of the things that makes this life work. The more you know how to do, the more jobs you can take. Until recently, I never really had to put much effort into finding work. I had a couple of big clients and all the work I wanted. This is now changing and I find myself becoming more a part of the gig economy, but because I have diverse skills, there are still lots of opportunities out there. I continue to maintain a home in Canada, but I rent it out when I'm away, so I can take long trips and go back and land contract work at the local TV stations when I need to.

HOW DID YOU MAKE MONEY?

At the beginning it was tough. I'd saved some money, but not enough. I was also carrying some debt, so even if I lived in a place with low costs, I still had to make 'real' money to pay my bills back home. For a while, I turned a blind eye and increased my debt load – I wouldn't recommend that.

Because I'd worked in the relatively small Canadian television industry, I had a broad professional network and, in the early days, work came to me. But with cutbacks in the media and increased competition, I'm having to work more just to find the work and the jobs are of shorter duration and pay less. House sitting has helped reduce my costs, but there are days when I wonder if this will continue to be sustainable.

HOW DO YOU MAKE THINGS WORK ON THE ROAD?

A few years ago, I did a piece on house sitting and it opened my eyes. I'd looked after animals and houses for friends in Canada, but suddenly I was seeing all these amazing long-term house-sits abroad listed on various websites.

The first one I snagged was for several months near Galway, Ireland, and to rent a place would have been prohibitive. However, in exchange for looking after two cats, I was given a comfortable house to live in for several months at no cost. Not having to pay housing costs takes the pressure off. Over the last few years, I've spent long periods house-sitting in Canada, Guatemala, Ireland and Scotland.

WHAT ADVICE WOULD YOU GIVE SOMEONE THINKING OF DOING THE SAME THING?

I've spent over a decade travelling and working online. I may not be getting rich, but I've had amazing experiences and I wouldn't trade it for the world. Try to line up jobs before you go. Save up some money as a buffer, don't carry any debt, and always keep learning. Network, network, network and don't be shy about marketing yourself.

Steve Waters

Steve Waters, travel writer and Database Administration Manager for Lonely Planet.

WHAT INSPIRED YOU TO TAKE YOUR JOB ON THE ROAD?

I've always been a traveller, and even before the tech revolution of the 2000s, I'd lived and worked in eight different cities across the globe. The advent of fast-internet, wi-fi and smartphones removed the need to be anchored in a specific city, so now I can work from (almost) anywhere. Providing IT support from the road involves frequent check-ins, so I always carry a smart-phone and laptop. If something comes up, I'll hole-up in one place until problems are resolved, and I always advise the company when I'll be uncontactable.

WHERE DO YOU NORMALLY WORK FROM?

Accommodation usually works best, followed by cafes, libraries and visitor centres. I've also worked from my vehicle when I've had cellphone reception, including once parked beside Vlamingh Head lighthouse while whales frolicked off Ningaloo Reef.

WHAT ARE THE BIGGEST CHALLENGES YOU'VE FACED ALONG THE WAY?

Easily the long distances and remoteness of Outback Australia, where hundreds of kilometres separate communities, and connections are via low-bandwidth satellite wi-fi, so you pay by the megabyte. Rough roads, insane heat, and millions of flies all add to the experience, and if you breakdown, there's bugger all phone reception to get rescued.

Once while working in the Kimberley I had a failing laptop battery which wouldn't charge and I'd also drowned my phone and DSLR. I ended up driving 600km to Darwin, where I got myself connected, worked for several hours to fix a Lonely Planet IT problem, then left again at sunrise and drove 600km back to the Kimberley, stopping only to buy a new phone in Katherine. In Iran I assumed I would be cut-off for a month but my corporate email worked while my personal email was blocked (and both were on Gmail). Telegram and Four Square rocked, Facebook and WhatsApp didn't. And forget internet banking: I travelled around with US$4000 in cash.

HAVE THE REALITIES OF REMOTE WORKING LIVED UP TO YOUR EXPECTATIONS?

Always! Sipping a beer, watching an eye-searing Indian Ocean sunset while working will always trump a windowless office. I'm also always amazed how connected other countries are – Nepal, Argentina, Iran, Russia all have plentiful and free wi-fi that puts regional Australia to shame.

HOW EASY HAVE YOU FOUND IT TO PLUG INTO LOCAL NOMAD COMMUNITIES?

Traveller camaraderie increases exponentially with the remoteness or difficulty of the travel. Most travellers these days are managing something online, be it work, a blog, or share trading. Congregate towards other travellers and you will find the nomads.

WHAT ADVICE WOULD YOU GIVE OTHER DIGITAL NOMADS?

Don't rely on old tech, upgrade everything before departure and ensure it all works. It's amazing how little things like batteries, chargers, software updates, banking, and banned social media applications can bring you unstuck. Good battery lifetime is essential!

Alex Reynolds

Alex Reynolds, travel blogger and Chief of Rambling at www.lostwithpurpose.com

WHY DID YOU BECOME A DIGITAL NOMAD?

After high school, I wanted to take a gap year, and my parents said 'hell, no', but my dreams were bigger than American two-week vacations. Things didn't become reality until seven years later. I was a graphic designer with itchy feet in the Netherlands, and this time there was no one to stop me.

WHAT WERE THE FIRST STEPS?

Travel requires money, so saving became my top priority. I sold everything except travel essentials at markets or online, and ended my apartment rental. My goal was to save $12,000 for one year of travel – beans and rice and Netflix replaced evenings out with friends. When quitting my job, I worked out an agreement with my old employer: the company would still use me for design projects. I think this step is essential. It's easier to get work from someone whom you've worked with before, and these clients are more likely to recommend you to others – hands-down the best way to find new clients.

Simultaneously, I built a travel blog. I hadn't heard of travel blogging before planning my travels, but I learned it could be profitable and I was intrigued. Photography, design, coding, marketing, wasting time on Instagram – it all seemed up my alley, and what did I have to lose? If I failed, it would at least save my mind from atrophying, and success meant living the dream of making money by travelling. Three years later, since I'm not dead, I'd say I'm moderately successful.

HOW DO YOU FIND WORK ON THE ROAD?

Clients old and new regularly request work, enough that I have the luxury of saying 'no', and my blog earns a regular pittance via ads, affiliates, and assignments. If one of my income streams suffers for whatever reason – a bad time of year, lack of clients, technical issues – I can rely on others to put food on my plate.

But it isn't easy. Regular income is a recent accomplishment, and balancing travel and work has been a constant struggle. Travelling to off-the-beaten track destinations means spending as much time looking for a signal as working. And being a female digital nomad in a male-dominated field, I suffer patronising men who assume the only way I make money online is by selling my bum on Instagram.

HAS THE LIFESTYLE LIVED UP TO YOUR EXPECTATIONS?

Is this "the dream"? Yes and no. I'm happy, but often stressed. Travel dreams are often complicated realities. I've hitchhiked for days down one of the highest roads in the world for a Skype call. I've climbed up mountains just to send emails. Some days I want to chuck my electronics off a cliff. More often, I'm in love with the life I created. Whether or not my nomadism is sustainable long-term, I have no regrets.

WHAT ADVICE WOULD YOU GIVE SOMEONE THINKING OF DOING THE SAME THING?

Lay the groundwork before departure. Set up your business, find clients, and build up enough savings. If you've already found your work groove it's easier to stay on track. A traditional nomad would never set off into the unknown without preparation; neither should a digital one.

Resources

Your quick-reference A–Z guide to the apps and websites mentioned in this book, and more.

ACCOMMODATION

Apartments & Rooms for Rent
Airbnb (www.airbnb.com)
GoBeHere (www.gobehere.com)
HolidayLettings (www.holidaylettings.com)
HomeAway (www.homeaway.com)
Nomad Rental (www.nomadrental.com)

Co-Living
CoLiving (www.coliving.com)
Digital Nomad House (www.digitalnomadhouse.net)
Outside (www.outsite.co)

Couchsurfing
Couchsurfing.com (www.couchsurfing.com).

Hostels & Hotels
Booking.com (www.booking.com)
HostelWorld.com (www.hostelworld.com)
Hotel Tonight (www.hoteltonight.com)
Hotels.com (www.hotels.com)
TripAdvisor (www.tripadvisor.com)

House-sitting
Housecarers (www.housecarers.com)
House Sitting World (www.housesittingworld.com)
MindMyHouse (www.mindmyhouse.com)

APPS FOR STAYING SAFE
BSafe (www.getbsafe.com)
CDC Apps (www.cdc.gov)
CityMapper (www.citymapper.com)
ICE – In Case of Emergency (Sylvian Lagache)
Offline Survival Manual (Ligi)
SmartTraveler (http://travel.state.gov)

APPS FOR TRAVEL
Facebook (www.facebook.com)
Instagram (www.instagram.com)
Livetrekker (www.livetrekker.com)
Skype (www.skype.com)
Rebtel (www.rebtel.com)
Toggl (www.toggl.com)
Touchnote (www.touchnote.com)
Tripcast (www.tripcast.co)
TripIt (www.tripit.com)
Viber (www.viber.com)
WhatsApp (www.whatsapp.com)

BLOGGING

Platforms
Blogger (www.blogger.com)
Constant Contact (www.constantcontact.com/website/builder)
Gator (www.hostgator.com/website-builder)
Wordpress.com (www.wordpress.com)
Wordpress.org (www.wordpress.org)

Tools
Gimp (www.gimp.org)
Google Analytics (https://analytics.google.com)
Google Docs (https://docs.google.com)
Google Keyword Planner (https://ads.google.com)
JPEGMini (www.jpegmini.com)
Yoast for Wordpress (www.yoast.com)

Promotion
Amazon Associates (www.affiliate-program.amazon.com)
Google AdSense (www.google.com/adsense)
Infolinks (www.infolinks.com)
Media.net (www.media.net)

FINDING WORK

General Job Sites

CareerBuilder (www.careerbuilder.com)
Flexjobs (www.flexjobs.com)
Fiverr (www.fiverr.com)
Freelancer (www.freelancer.com)
Indeed (www.indeed.com)
Monster (www.monster.com)
People Per Hour (www.peopleperhour.com)
Reed (www.reedglobal.com)
Remote (www.remote.co)
We Work Remotely (www.weworkremotely.com)
Working Nomads (www.workingnomads.co)
Upwork (www.upwork.com)

Editing

ProEdit (www.proedit.com)
Scribbr (www.scribbr.com)
Society for Editors & Proofreaders
    (www.sfep.org.uk)
Writing English (www.writingenglish.com)

Developer Tools

Arc (www.arc.dev)
Code Mentor (www.codementor.io)
Dzone (www.dzone.com)
Freelancer's Union (www.freelancersunion.org)
GitHub (www.github.com)
Just Remote (www.justremote.co)
RemoteOK (www.remoteok.io)
Stack Overflow (www.stackoverflow.com)

Graphic Design

99 Designs (www.99designs.co.uk)
AngelList (www.angel.co)
Creative Market (www.creativemarket.com)
Freepik (www.freepik.com)

Music

Audio Jungle (www.audiojungle.net)
Pond 5 (www.pond5.com)
Premium Beat (www.premiumbeat.com)

Photography

123RF (www.123rf.com)

500Px (https://web.500px.com)
Alamy (www.alamy.com)
Bigstock (www.bigstockphoto.com)
Getty Images (www.gettyimages.co.uk)
iStock (www.istockphoto.com)
Shutterstock (www.shutterstock.com)

Support Jobs, SEO & Marketing

Adbrands (www.adbrands.net)
Buzzsumo (www.buzzsumo.com)
Facebook Audience Insights
   (www.facebook.com/ads/audience_insights)
Google Analytics (https://analytics.google.com)
Search Engine Land (www.searchengineland.com)
SEO Round Table (www.seroundtable.com)
The Beginner's Guide to SEO from Moz (https://
   moz.com/beginners-guide-to-seo)
Twitter Analytics (https://analytics.twitter.com)
Virtual Assistant Handbook
   (www.thevahandbook.com)

Teaching & Translation

Cambly (www.cambly.com)
CourseFinders (www.coursefinders.com)
English Hunt (www.englishhuntusa.com)

Duolingo (www.duolingo.com)
Freelancer (www.freelancer.com)
Google Translate (https://translate.google.com)
iTranslate (www.itranslate.com)
NiceTalk (http://tutor.nicetalk.com)
One Hour Translation (www.onehourtranslation.
   com)
Palfish (www.ipalfish.com)
ProZ (www.proz.com)
QKids (https://teacher.qkids.net)
SayABC (https://t.sayabc.com)
Tandem (www.tandem.net)
TEFL (Teaching English as a Foreign Language;
   www.tefl.org)
TESOL (Teaching English to Speakers of Other
   Language; www.tesol.org)
Translate (www.translate.com/translators)
TripLingo (www.triplingo.com)
UnBabel (www.unbabel.com)
VipKid (https://t.vipkid.com.cn)

Videography

Adobe Stock (https://stock.adobe.com)
Shutterstock (www.shutterstock.com)
Pond5 (www.pond5.com)

Web Design & Web Development
Adobe (www.adobe.com)
Adobe Portfolio (https://portfolio.adobe.com)
Behance (www.behance.net)
Codeacademy (www.codeacademy.com)
Coroflot (www.coroflot.com)
freeCodeCamp (www.freecodecamp.org)
Dribbble (www.dribbble.com)
SkillCrush (www.skillcrush.com)

Writing Resources
Creativepool (www.creativepool.com)
Freelance Writing (www.freelancewriting.com)
Lonely Planet (www.lonelyplanet.com)
OnlineNewpaperList
  (www.onlinenewspaperlist.com)
The Culture Trip (www.theculturetrip.com)
The Write Life (www.thewritelife.com)

GENERAL NOMAD RESOURCES

Cloud Storage
DropBox (www.dropbox.com)
Google Drive (www.google.com/drive)

Co-Working Spaces
CoWorker (www.coworker.com)
Croissant (www.getcroissant.com)

Destination Guides & Nomad Resources
Chris the Freelancer (www.christhefreelancer.com)
Entrepreneur (www.entrepreneur.com)
Nomad Gate (www.nomadgate.com)
Nomad List (www.nomadlist.com)

Networking
Facebook (www.facebook.com)
Google Meet (https://meet.google.com)
Instagram (www.instagram.com)
LinkedIn (www.linkedin.com)
Meetup (www.meetup.com)
Pinterest (www.pinterest.com)
Slack (www.slack.com)

Trello (www.trello.com)
Twitter (www.twitter.com)
Vimeo (www.vimeo.com)
YouTube (www.youtube.com)

Virtual Private Networks
Express VPN (www.expressvpn.com)
Nord VPN (www.nordvpn.com)

Wi-Fi & Internet Access
Boingo (www.boingo.com)
Flexiroam (www.flexiroam.com)
OpenWiFiSpots (www.openwifispots.com)
WiFi Free Spot (www.wififreespot.com)
WiFi Map (www.wifimap.io)
Wiman (www.wiman.me)

MONEY

Apps for Money
Splittr (www.splittr.io)
Starling (www.starlingbank.com)
Trabee Pocket (www.trabeepocket.com)
WeSwap (www.weswap.com)
XE (www.xe.com)

Accounting & Taxes
Evernote (www.evernote.com)
Freshbooks (www.freshbooks.com)
Harvest (www.getharvest.com)
Quickbooks (https://quickbooks.intuit.com)
Worldwide Personal Tax and Immigration guide
  from Ernst & Young (search on www.ey.com)

Payment Tools
Apple Pay (www.apple.com/uk/apple-pay)
Azimo (www.azimo.com)
Caxton FX (www.caxtonfx.com)
FairFX (www.fairfx.com)
Google Pay (https://pay.google.com)
Moneygram (www.moneygram.com)
OFX (www.ofx.com).
Paypal (www.paypal.com)

Revolut (www.revolut.com)
Transferwise (www.transferwise.com)
Western Union (www.westernunion.com)

TRAVEL ADVISORY INFORMATION

Australian Department of Foreign Affairs & Trade
   (www.smartraveller.gov.au)
Foreign & Commonwealth Office
   (www.gov.uk/foreign-travel-advice)
New Zealand Department of Foreign Affairs &
   Trade (www.safetravel.govt.nz)
US State Department (http://travel.state.gov)

TRAVEL HEALTH

Allergy Translation (www.allergytranslation.com)
Centres for Disease Control & Prevention
   (https://wwwnc.cdc.gov/travel)
Dr Deb, the Travel Doctor

(www.thetraveldoctor.com.au)
Fight the Fakes (www.fightthefakes.org)
Select Wisely (www.selectwisely.com)
Travel Health Pro (www.travelhealthpro.org.uk)

TRAVEL INSURANCE

Safety Wing (www.safetywing.com)
True Traveller (www.truetraveller.com)
World Nomads (www.worldnomads.com)

TRANSPORT

Organised Nomad Trips
Hacker Paradise (www.hackerparadise.org)
Remote Year (www.remoteyear.com)
WiFi Tribe (www.wifitribe.co)

Taxi Hailing Apps
Curb (https://mobileapp.gocurb.com)

– North America
Didi Chuxing (www.didiglobal.com) – China
GrabTaxi (www.grab.com) – Southeast Asia
Line (www.linecorp.com) – Japan
Lyft (www.lyft.com) – North America
Ola (www.olacabs.com) – India
Uber (www.uber.com) – worldwide

Transport
Aviation Safety Network (www.aviation-safety.net)
Expedia (www.expedia.com)
Ferrylines (www.ferrylines.com)
Google Maps (https://maps.google.com)
Hipmunk (www.hipmunk.com)
Kayak (www.kayak.co.uk)
OneWorld (www.oneworld.com)
Rome2Rio (www.rome2rio.com)
Skiplagged (www.skiplagged.com)
Skyscanner (www.skyscanner.net)
SkyTeam (www.skyteam.com)
Star Alliance (www.staralliance.com)
The Flight Deal (www.theflightdeal.com)
The Man in Seat 61 (www.seat61.com)
Travel Pirates (www.travelpirates.com)
TravelZoo (www.travelzoo.com)

TRAVEL OFFSETTING
Climate Action Reserve
(www.climateactionreserve.org)
Gold Standard (www.goldstandard.org)
Plan Vivo (www.planvivo.org)
Verra (www.verra.org)

VISAS
Australian Working Holiday (https://immi.
homeaffairs.gov.au/visas/getting-a-visa/visa-
listing/work-holiday-417)
Best Onward Ticket (www.bestonwardticket.com)
Costa Rica Rentista Visas
(www.migracion.go.cr/Paginas/Visas)
Estonia e-Residency (www.e-resident.gov.ee)

Estonia Start-up Visa (www.startupestonia.ee).
Germany Freiberufler & Selbständiger Visas
(https://service.berlin.de/dienstleistung/305249/
en)
Mexico Residente Temporal Visa
(www.gob.mx/tramites/ficha/visa-de-residencia-
temporal/SRE260)
One Way Fly (www.onewayfly.com)
Thailand's Hand-to-Hand Combat Visa (www.mfa.
go.th/main/en/services)
Visa List (www.visalist.io)

INDEX

NOTES

Published in April 2020 by Lonely Planet Global Limited
CRN 554153
www.lonelyplanet.com
ISBN 978 1 83869 042 7
© Lonely Planet 2020
Printed in China
10 9 8 7 6 5 4 3 2 1

Publishing Director Piers Pickard
Associate Publisher Robin Barton
Editors Dora Ball, Polly Thomas
Art Director Daniel Di Paolo
Layout Diana Jarvis
Picture Research Regina Wolek
Proofreading Karyn Noble
Print Production Nigel Longuet
Cover illustration © Muti / Folio Art
Thanks to Flora MacQueen, Christina Webb

Written by Joe Bindloss

STAY IN TOUCH lonelyplanet.com/contact

AUSTRALIA The Malt Store, Level 3, 551 Swanston St, Carlton, Victoria 3053. T: 03 8379 8000

IRELAND Digital Depot, Roe Lane (off Thomas St), Digital Hub, Dublin 8, D08 TCV4

USA Suite 208, 155 Filbert Street, Oakland, CA94607. T: 510 250 6400

UNITED KINGDOM 240 Blackfriars Rd, London SE1 8NW. T: 020 3771 5100

Paper in this book is certified against the Forest Stewardship Council™ standards. FSC™ promotes environmentally responsible, socially beneficial and economically viable management of the world's forests.